Hot Chocolate *in* June

Endorsement

HOT CHOCOLATE IN JUNE is full of sweet surprises! Holly Mthethwa has delivered a heartwarming, heart-wrenching, heartfelt series of raw and real stories that will bring you to laughter and tears. You will be moved, challenged, and encouraged by Holly's journey of faith. I certainly was.

—ELLIE LOFARO

Author, Speaker, and International Bible Teacher

Hot Chocolate *in* June

A True Story of Loss, Love and Restoration

HOLLY MTHETHWA

AMBASSADOR INTERNATIONAL
GREENVILLE, SOUTH CAROLINA & BELFAST, NORTHERN IRELAND

www.ambassador-international.com

Hot Chocolate in June
A Story of Loss, Love and Restoration

Printed in the United States of America

ISBN: 978-1-62020-256-2
eISBN: 978-1-62020-356-9

Cover design and typesetting: Matthew Mulder
E-book conversion: Anna Riebe

AMBASSADOR INTERNATIONAL
Emerald House
427 Wade Hampton Blvd.
Greenville, SC 29609, USA
www.ambassador-international.com

AMBASSADOR BOOKS
The Mount
2 Woodstock Link
Belfast, BT6 8DD, Northern Ireland, UK
www.ambassadormedia.co.uk

The colophon is a trademark of Ambassador

To my Jesus:

For your rescue of me, for your growing me, for your pursuit of me.

For your glory!

All that I am and am to be is because of you.

To my husband, to you Oscar:

Your love for me defies the bounds of reason, and flows from a place none other than Heaven. Your passion for God has and will always bring me to my knees, begging for more. Thank you for believing in me. You bring such joy to my life. I love you!

For you, Dad

Table of Contents

Acknowledgements

Acknowledgement:
recognition of the importance of something or someone.

FIRST, I RECOGNIZE YOU, LORD Jesus. I acknowledge Your importance in the orchestration of this book. These words are yours; may You use them, may they be effective for You. I'm blown over by your grace; and I thank You from the depths of my heart for it. I acknowledge You.

My hubby, thank you for putting up with take-aways, cereal for dinner, unwashed laundry, and a wife too often lost in thought while I was writing this. Thank you for the endless coffees, hugs, words of encouragement, and prayers over this book. Your selflessness throughout this process has shown me the grace of Jesus time and time again. I acknowledge you a thousand times over.

Mom, for Christmas 2012 you gave me *The Christian Writer's Market Guide*, with an inscription on the inside cover which read, "You have a gift. God has a plan for you so continue to pursue the desire He has placed within your heart." I recognize your importance in all of this, in all of me. Thank you for your belief in me and your prayers for me. Thank you for letting me write, as I felt led, without fear of embarrassment. I acknowledge you.

Jim, to the step-dad who stepped in as a dad, I hope I don't embarrass you too much within these pages. You have cared for me, provided for me, assisted me, and loved me like your very own daughter—I am your daughter. I know that your concern for me has and always will be out of a deep love within your heart—and I thank you for that! I acknowledge you.

Ma Mary and Dad Cornelius, thank you for accepting me into your family. Thank you for loving me as your own daughter—for putting aside our cultural and racial differences and for showing me love. I'm so grateful that God chose you to be my mother-in-law and father-in-law; you've taught me so much. I acknowledge you.

To my brothers, one full, one half, some step—some not-so-step anymore—you're all my brothers: Danny, Jakob, Jason, Darren, Dale, Zach, and Jeff, you guys provide a life full of so much fun and laughter! I'm always filled with joy when I'm around you. Thank you for liking me. I acknowledge you.

To my one and only sister, Bailey, thank you for being so patient and forgiving with me as I've grown into my big sister role over the years. I am more thankful for you than you'll ever know. Your fierceness keeps me on my toes and your tenderness keeps me on my knees. I acknowledge you.

Angie, thank you for caring for Dad; for stepping out in faith; for teaching me about Jesus through your actions. You truly are an angel, and I acknowledge you.

Erin, thank you for stepping in to be a mother to me while you were with Dad. Thank you for your effort in allowing us to keep the family together even after your separation and his death. I acknowledge you for the role you've played.

Grandma Rose, thank you for sweet and gentle love; for your unconditional acceptance. I always loved seeing your books laying out on the coffee table and your coffee cup sitting next to them. I acknowledge you.

Grandma Alberts, thank you for always being excited and interested in what your grandchildren are doing and for always being involved. I acknowledge you.

Jenna, my best friend and cousin, thank you for always listening to my poems and writing. Thank you for being brave enough to act out the adventurous stories I'd concoct in my head when we were little girls. Thank you for being deeply saddened when my writing ceased, and for being brought to tears of joy when the Lord brought me to a place where I could write again. I acknowledge you.

Jamie Vasconcelos and Heather Wellman, thank you for reading this book before it was finished and before it was a published book. Thank you for your encouragement, your guidance, and your wisdom. Thank you for the time you devoted to ensure that this dream would become a reality. I acknowledge you.

My publishers, Sam and Tim Lowry, and the Ambassador International team, thank you for choosing this book. Thank you for this opportunity and for believing in the power of a testimony and a story told. You have assisted God in making one of my deepest desires come true. I acknowledge you.

My editor, J.P. Brooks: when one of your first words to me was "LOL," I knew that this was an ordained partnership. Thank you for your input, your resources, your expertise, your humor, and your prayers for this book. You are a truly gifted editor and you have provided invaluable guidance. Your divinely inspired suggestions and wordsmithing have made this book all the better. I acknowledge you.

To all the people, all my family and friends, named and unnamed, who've helped me get to this point—to this point in my walk with Christ and to this point in the completion of this book—I acknowledge you. You've been so important, so crucial.

Introduction

"I am a tree, in a story about a forest. And the story of the forest is better than the story of the tree."

Paraphrased from Donald Miller's book
A Million Miles in a Thousand Years

Give thanks to the Lord, call on His name; make known among the nations what He has done, and proclaim that His name is exalted. Sing to the Lord, for He has done glorious things; let this be known to all the world.

– Isaiah 12:4–5

THIS BOOK WAS WRITTEN TO do exactly what the above verse proclaims, "to make known among the nations what He has done." I have no desire to write a book merely about me and my experiences, but about what wonderful things God has done through me and in me. As I make known among the nations what He has done in my life, it is my prayer that it will encourage all who read to also share their stories. May our stories, our testimonies, rise up from the depths of the earth and exalt His name.

CHAPTER ONE

"Goodbye, Pumpkin"

I DROVE.

The crisp, fall Nebraska air blew so strongly, with threats of winter frost, that neither the warmth of the heater nor sips from the cappuccino in my cup holder could melt its chilling effects. I was headed west along Interstate 80 in my white 2004 Oldsmobile Alero, toward the seasonally abandoned cornfields of Cozad, Nebraska. The night sky intensified my eagerness to get home. It was Thanksgiving break, during my second year of college, and school had let out early, but a part-time job had kept me from making the forty-five-minute drive home until nightfall.

My parents divorced when I was six yet still, at the age of nineteen, I spent every other holiday between the two of them. Having outgrown the requirements of the divorce decree, I was at the age where I could simply decide whom I wanted to spend a holiday with, but something about choosing felt disloyal; wrong. So I headed toward Dad's house and my hometown, because, well, Thanksgiving was his turn this year.

Long ago, my brother Danny and I determined to make the best out of our situation. We discovered that children of divorced parents not only get to celebrate each holiday three times more than other kids, but they also get three times as many Christmas presents come Christmas time. When you're a kid and you start multiplying your anticipated gifts by two parents, two step-parents, two sets of grandparents, two sets of step-grandparents, and step-siblings, it becomes easy to find the silver lining in being the by-product of divorce. If your step-parents' parents are also divorced, like ours were, then you throw in a couple more sets of grandparents and you've got yourself your own toy store. We knew the true purpose of Christmas wasn't found in the gifts, but I guess as a child one tends to always look for the good in situations. At nineteen, however, this "good" typically just meant I gained three times more weight than the young adult who had less holiday functions to attend and thus less food to encounter.

As a child, I don't remember wishing my parents would get back together more than a handful of times. Mom sat down with me one evening while I was brushing my Barbie doll's hair and told me that she and Dad were going to get divorced, which meant they were going to separate and she would go and live in another house. She said my brother and I would also come live with her if a judge, who had to sort out the process, decided it was best. We would have two homes and it would be better for her and Dad, as well as for me and Danny, who was three years old at the time. I guess I believed her. A funny thing happened though: a weird, angry feeling, mixed with a pain inside my heart, washed over me like water in a shower. I wasn't sad and I didn't cry. I'd never felt this feeling before. Barbie dropped to the floor with a plastic clatter; my feet pattered across the bathroom tiles as I rushed out of the room, and my six-year-old heart had its first encounter with the feeling of betrayal.

I sped to the living room, picked up the handset to our black, rotary dial telephone and dunked my tiny fingers into the circle above each digit of my grandma's phone number. It seemed like an eternity as I rolled the dial to the metal stopper, waited for it to roll back, and entered the rest of the numbers. I had memorized Grandma Rose's number in case of an emergency, and this felt like an emergency. Grandma Rose was Dad's Mom, and I loved her. My parents might be leaving each other, but I was leaving them first.

After Grandma agreed to pick me up, I shoved Barbie and pajamas in my pleasant, pink suitcase, which had *Going to Grandma's* printed on the front, with the image of a little girl walking alongside a white picket fence, holding a lunch box and books in her hand. It was my favorite suitcase and I thought it was perfect, especially since I was going to Grandma's. Once everything I needed was packed, I flipped the hook up, then back down to lock it, headed out the door, and waited outside on the sidewalk until my grandma's Buick pulled up. I refused to talk to Mom or Dad.

Running away only lasted for the night. By morning, I had forgiven my parents and gone back to brushing Barbie's hair: eventually in two homes. Later, I even went on to have a full Barbie doll collection at both homes, so I didn't have to cart them in my suitcase between visitations. It wasn't so bad, and here I sat, thirteen years later, driving back to Cozad to celebrate Thanksgiving with Dad.

After I arrived home that evening, I lay on the floor of what used to be my brother's room. I was surrounded by solar system wallpaper proudly stained with neon paintball splashes (the aftermath of Danny perfecting his once-new hobby), and a large Batman nightlight. The day I went off to college, Danny excitedly moved all his stuff—well, basically just the stuff he wanted to move—into my room, leaving me in the leftovers of his boyhood sanctuary on my weekends at Dad's. I lay there reading the book *When God Writes Your Love Story*, thinking about failed past relationships of mine, and desperate for this God-written love story the authors depicted. Dad slowly opened the door, looked down at me with his sky-blue eyes and whispered, "Goodnight, Pumpkin."

"Goodnight, Dad. Love you," I replied.

I kept reading. I had grown up thinking I loved Jesus, but it was only the year before this, during my first year at college, when I really began to understand what that meant. I didn't even know God wrote love stories. I mean, I knew He was in control, but I didn't think He spent that much time in the details of a person's life. I thought He was too busy solving world problems and keeping the universe aligned. But I was beginning to believe these authors might be on to something, and that God truly could write the most amazing love story: a fairy tale, even. So, as I drifted off to sleep, tucked warmly beneath a crocheted afghan, I began telling God exactly how I wanted Him to write my love story, and what characters should be involved. (Too funny, right? Reading a book on allowing God to be the sole author of my love story instead of me trying to write it, and my immediate reaction is . . . to start telling Him how to write it! I bet the Father and Jesus had a good chuckle over that one.)

The next day we celebrated Thanksgiving, which consisted of lunch at Grandma Rose's house and dinner at my step-grandma's house. I remember sitting at my step-grandma's kitchen table with her and my step-mom, sipping coffee, and listening to them talk about God. The two of them both loved God, and I was grateful for that. I was still learning about God, so I sat there listening and staring out the window. I spent that night on the floor beneath the afghan again, delving even deeper into my book. I couldn't get it out of my head: even the title said *when* God writes your love story, not *if* God writes it. This made it seem like He was prepared to write everyone's, if everyone would only let Him.

The morning after Thanksgiving, Danny, who was sixteen at the time, and I were up early packing our bags and getting ready to head to Mom's house in Doniphan, Nebraska. Though the holiday was Dad's, it was technically Mom's weekend, and we had an hour-and-fifteen-minute drive ahead of us. Dad kindly helped load my car and handed me twenty dollars for gas. Dad was always handing me twenty-dollar bills for things. Once, in middle school, I'd gotten my heart broken by a boy. When Dad picked me up from track practice and saw my tears, he reached into his worn-out, black leather billfold, pulled out a twenty and said, "Here, maybe this will help." Never much for words, it was his way of showing me he cared. Surprisingly, once I got over the initial tears, it did kind of help.

With everything ready to go, Dad kissed my forehead saying, "Goodbye, Pumpkin. I love you." Had I only known those were the last words I would ever hear him say, or the last time I'd ever be called "Pumpkin," I would have lingered a little longer. Pumpkin was Dad's nickname for me. No one else ever called me Pumpkin; only Dad.

The drive to Mom's was nothing out of the ordinary. We took our usual route, Interstate 80, this time driving back east. Danny and I were close, so we talked and listened to music. When he reclined in his seat, tipped his cap over his eyes and fell asleep, I got lost in my own thoughts.

I thought about Danny and what potential he had. Mom always said he would be a preacher one day. It took a few years after her divorce from Dad, but Mom had also grown closer to God. She had started taking us to Victory Bible Fellowship every weekend we were with her and talking to us about following Jesus. Most people laughed when Mom told them about Danny's future career. Others politely nodded, then walked away from the conversation, thinking she was half crazy. You see, Danny had been getting into trouble for as long as I could remember. I don't know how many phone calls Dad had gotten from the police station asking him to come down and get Danny. Not only that, but Danny had a fancy for illegal substances. Some that were illegal due to him being underage, and others simply because they were illegal.

I glanced over at him while he slept, and I believed what Mom said. Deep down, Danny had the best heart of anyone I knew. The problem was, the best part was deep down—and not everyone could see that far.

Danny and I had been at Mom's for just a few hours when we got a phone call from Grandma Rose. She was distraught, but with some deciphering we picked up what she was saying.

"Your Dad was out chopping wood," her voice trembled uncontrollably.

"He took a lunch break and started choking on his food, and lost all movement on his right side. We think he had a stroke, and he's being airlifted to the hospital in Lincoln."

My heart sank. "We'll be right there."

Lincoln was a two-and-a-half-hour drive east from Cozad, and it had one of the state's biggest hospitals. Mom drove Danny and me. Since we were already farther east, it would take us only about an hour to get there.

Sitting in the passenger seat as Mom drove to the hospital was like sitting on a plane to an unknown destination. Thoughts raced through my mind. My body quivered as if the blood pulsing through my veins was cold. I kept thinking of scriptures I'd read over the last year and a half, reassuring myself that God was in control and He would use this for good, yet there was a nagging feeling in my heart that my definition of good and God's definition might not be quite the same.

The hospital stood beckoning as we approached, like the darkened towers of a deserted castle. I was being pulled toward the entrance with the conflicting emotions of wanting—and at the same time not wanting—to see what awaited us inside. We walked into the room where Dad was. He was flat on his back, between the white sheets of the hospital bed, in the emergency room, tears welling up in the corners of his eyes. I looked right into his eyes and saw a deep-set fear I'd never seen before. I began to talk to him. He stared back at me. It was then Grandma Rose whispered, "He can't speak; he hasn't been able to since it happened." I knew she was scared.

Her eldest son, Dad's only sibling, my Uncle Steve, had passed away just two years prior from brain cancer. Uncle Steve had been forty-two. Dad was forty-two this year. I knew those thoughts were in the back of Grandma's mind and my dad's mind. They were in the back of all of our minds.

A couple of hours later, scans and tests revealed that a spot in Dad's brain was bleeding, causing the stroke-like symptoms of lost speech and paralysis on the right side of his body. Dad's condition became immensely worse during the night; so much so, that the next morning the doctors suggested immediate brain surgery to try to stop the bleeding. We agreed. Of course we agreed.

Numbness overtook me—the kind of numbness that makes you feel like you're floating in an alternate universe, experiencing everything from outside your body. I cried out to God the best I knew how and asked Him what He was thinking, but surprisingly, I wasn't yet angry. There was a still, quiet resolve within. I knew I needed to trust this God I'd been getting to know.

After his surgery, I stepped into Dad's cold, white-walled room in the intensive care unit. An antiseptic smell burned my nostrils, and the sight before my eyes was seared into my heart. My father lay there with a ventilator forcing him to breathe. Drain tubes protruded from his freshly shaven and bandaged head. I nearly collapsed when I heard the in-and-out sound of the ventilator. His breathing— which used to echo through our house while he slept: like the in-and-out growl of a grizzly bear—had become a machine-automated, crisp click.

Not long after his surgery, we met with the doctors. The only part of what they said that day that I remember was the part I feared hearing the most. While they were working inside Dad's brain, patching up the bleeding, they found a spot of abnormal tissue. They weren't quite sure what it was, but were sending it to Pathology and we would know in a few days. That was all. We could only wait.

By this time, Grandma Rose, Danny, Mom, my cousins who were Uncle Steve's kids: Jamie, Jenna, and Jarod; my step-mom, Angie, and my step-brothers, Jeff and Zach, were all at the hospital. Over the years Dad had been divorced twice, and my first step-mom and now Dad's second ex-wife (don't worry if you're confused, I get lost, too) had also arrived with my youngest brother Jakob, who was four at the time. If Dad could've seen the waiting room, I imagine it would have made him a bit uncomfortable. It was complicated: two ex-wives and his current wife all huddled in the gloomy waiting room. Surprisingly, there was no animosity. These three women knew their children needed to be there; besides, none of them really had a problem with each other. Their problem had been their own marriage to Dad.

Mom (which one, you might ask), eventually went back to Doniphan. Most of the rest of us slept in the waiting room, pushing together chairs and footrests to create make-shift beds. Danny and I didn't say much about what was going on. I knew he was hurting and wanted to escape it all. Little Jakob also didn't fully understand. He just knew Daddy was sick, like Uncle Steve had been, and didn't look the same.

For the next week, we lived in Bryan Memorial Hospital. The smell of antiseptics replaced the fresh smell of the open plains. We ate prepackaged food in the hospital cafeteria. We watched the hospital's TV. We anxiously paced the hospital's bleak halls. Friends and family came and went, but we remained. The only time we left was to shower at friends' houses. I didn't really care if I showered. Greasy hair no longer seemed to matter. If I smelled like unwashed scalp and stale sweat, it might keep people from approaching, which would do me a service, as I had no desire to talk to anyone.

Since Dad had lost his ability to swallow, the doctor punctured a hole in his pudgy abdomen and inserted a feeding tube. A medium-sized plastic tube ran from his abdomen up into a plastic bag that hung, along with multiple other bags, from a stainless steel IV pole. I'd sit in Dad's room and stare at the thick, peach-colored goo, thinking "thank goodness that bypasses his taste buds and goes straight into his stomach." Dad loved his hamburgers and Pepsi; from the looks of the mush in that bag, it wouldn't have tasted like either.

Finally, the pathology results came back. I inhaled deeply and held my breath as the doctors announced that the abnormal tissue in Dad's brain was malignant melanoma: a big word just to describe cancer. My ears rang with the sound of clanging cymbals as I heard them say words like "treatment," "rehabilitation," "more tests," and "advanced stage." I faded out of the conversation. The first free moment I got, I rode the elevator to the room that housed a computer, a number of floors above the ICU floor.

My fingers shook as I typed the diagnosis into Google. I read every article I could find, only to be filled with the knowledge that, according to statistics, most people with this type of cancer, at this stage, live for only six months to a year after diagnosis. I had never known melanoma to be so serious. I thought skin cancer could be easily removed, and then the person could go on living their life wearing sunscreen. My father, with his blue eyes, fair skin, and strawberry red hair had been more prone to melanoma than others.

As we had feared, the cancer was in his brain; but there was more. The doctor said the cancer would have started out on his skin and spread to his brain, so more than likely it was also elsewhere. More tests.

Dad still couldn't talk. They told him he had cancer: all he could do was look between us and the doctor and shake his head that he understood. I wanted to hear what he had to say; what he would tell us. I knew he wouldn't have said much anyway because he never did, but I would have cherished the few words he would offer.

The test results came back. Though they were revealed to us with compassion, I knew they read like a fact sheet with intellectual words: cancer in brain, cancer in lymph nodes, tumors in abdomen, tumor on pancreas, tumor near liver. This wasn't a discolored and misshapen mole that could be removed. This was a vicious and fast-moving army, conquering his body organ by organ, as if it were some territory to be claimed.

We bought Dad a small dry-erase board and red whiteboard marker so he could try to communicate with us. The bleeding in Dad's brain didn't just cause him to lose his speech and ability to swallow, it paralyzed the entire right side of his body: from his droopy face to his limp right arm, all the way down to his unmovable right leg, Dad lost mobility. This strong man, who only days earlier had gripped the handle of his axe and in one fluid motion raised it over his shoulders to bring it crashing back down on the chopping block so we'd have firewood for winter, this strong man would now be swinging his body into a wheelchair. This couldn't happen to my dad. My dad was always strong; invincible. Accustomed to writing with his right hand and now having to write with his left, Dad's penmanship was legible, but poor. Watching him try to write, I could see the effects of his brain tumor manifesting themselves in more ways than just physically. The frustration in his eyes revealed what he couldn't say. At times, he couldn't remember the words to use to communicate. He would struggle stringing a sentence together. I'd look intently at him, but he would shake his head as embarrassment washed over his face, and his red marker would go down, defeated, in his lap.

I don't remember how long he was in the hospital before he was transferred to Madonna Rehabilitation Hospital, one of the nation's leading hospitals for rehabilitating patients with traumatic brain injuries—something the cancer in his brain had caused. This new hospital was also in Lincoln, so we didn't have to travel far. It must've been a couple of weeks before they moved him. I missed a week of school, returned to Kearney, my college town, the following week, then drove back to Lincoln on Friday, once I had finished work. The doctors decided it would be best for Dad to go through intense rehabilitation to try to re-learn how to swallow, speak, and walk before he began the treatment for cancer.

I remember driving into the facility, the ground covered in a blanket of snow, staring at the cars that filled the parking lot. It's funny what the human brain remembers, especially during traumatic events. Seven years later, I don't remember a lot about the rehabilitation hospital, but I specifically remember sitting in the parking lot eating tomato-and basil-flavored Wheat Thins. Angie, Dad's current wife, had introduced me to them and I couldn't get enough.

You likely know that individuals remember a smell or a detail of a specific event more than they remember the whole event. It's no surprise, then, that eating those Wheat Thins is one of my most vivid memories from the rehabilitation hospital. Perhaps it's the sheer insignificance of the event that makes it so significant. Either that, or I have an extreme obsession with food. Both could very well be equally true.

Dad worked with various therapists, each teaching him how to do things that had once come naturally to him. He, quite quickly, learned how to swallow again, allowing him to eat without relying solely on the feeding tube. As he was still learning, though, and unable to eat portions that would sustain him, the tube remained in. I knew he sometimes got frustrated, but Dad worked very hard. He had always been a hard worker and he had impressed upon me, at a young age, the importance of working hard. Dad was always very committed; he'd worked at the same company for twenty-plus years.

Grandma Rose and Angie stayed with Dad the entire time he was at the rehabilitation hospital. Danny and I would return to school during the week and drive back to Lincoln for the weekends. Some of the nights we stayed in family housing, close to the hospital, which was available to a patient's family at a lower cost than a hotel. On other nights we stayed at Angie's cousin's house.

One night, in particular, I remember leaving the hospital late to head to Angie's cousin's. Angie and I sat at the kitchen counter while her cousin ground fresh coffee beans. I can still hear the sound of the coffee grinder working, as I recall that night. I sat in the kitchen drinking coffee with them and I felt so at peace, so relaxed, so calm despite the circumstances. I have no doubt it was God's peace, God's mercy, I felt. As I sat there drinking coffee with those two beautiful souls, it was as if I also sat drinking coffee with the Prince of Peace, and He was telling me that no matter what happened, I would be okay. Whispering over me as I read, "Peace I leave with you; my peace I give you. I do not give to you as the world gives. Do not let your hearts be troubled and do not be afraid" (John 14:27).

Dad must've been in the rehabilitation hospital only two-and-a-half weeks, because shortly before Christmas the doctor made the statement that if it were him in Dad's place, he would want to spend what might be his last Christmas at home with his family. He strongly suggested we should consider bringing Dad home, and we took his advice. Dad would not be going back to Madonna.

The cancer was so far advanced, that I guess they thought for him to spend his last few months in rehabilitation was unnecessary. I wasn't there for a lot of those conversations, so I didn't know all the details surrounding every decision, but I knew that sending him home meant they believed he didn't have a lot of time.

Despite his early release from the rehabilitation hospital, Dad had fully re-learned how to swallow and could walk short distances with a cane and assistance. He still couldn't speak or move his right arm, but was able to make grunts and sounds.

Jakob made a "Welcome Home Dad" poster to hang in our living room for his arrival. With an alphabet repertoire consisting of the letters in his name and a few others, Jakob, of course, had had some help. Jakob, with the Kostman round cheeks and strawberry red hair, was the spitting image of Dad. His dark eyes, however, resembled the dark brown color of his mom's.

Once Dad was brought home from the hospital, Angie left her job to care for Dad, the man she loved. A hospital bed was brought into our house and since the only spare room was my room, we moved the bed in there. Instead of white-washed walls, Dad was now the one surrounded by splashes of neon colors, planets, and Batman. I thought it made for a warmer atmosphere, but I was once again kicked out of a bedroom and onto the couch. Sometimes I'd lie on the floor beside his hospital bed, praying he would be okay.

It reminded me of the nights I'd spent as a little girl on the floor in his room. When I was scared, I'd crawl into his room and lie on the floor beside his bed asking him to hang his arm over the edge so I could hold his hand until I fell asleep. He always did, and I'd soon fall asleep feeling safe with my hand in his. He used to tell me that everything was okay, but it was no longer okay, and he could no longer swing his arm over the side of the bed to hold my hand. I'd sit next to the hospital bed, take his hand in mine, and marvel at how life had changed. In my mind, this was not supposed to be. This was not supposed to happen.

Shortly after Christmas, Dad developed severe pain in his leg. Swollen and hot to the touch, we knew it could very well be a blood clot. As he wasn't as mobile as before, we'd been warned these might occur. Dad had worn compression socks since the beginning of the ordeal, to help prevent clots from developing, but it wasn't uncommon for one to form despite the measures taken.

We took him to the local clinic where it was suggested we take him to Kearney to have his leg examined more closely. Angie drove him down there. Danny and I had planned to celebrate a late Christmas with Mom and her side of the family, so we headed to the tiny town of Elwood, to my aunt's house, about thirty minutes away.

Mom is the fifth of six children, making family get-togethers anything but small, and nothing if not chaotic. Each of the six siblings has two to three children, some of whom have two to three children of their own, ensuring that when we come together the numbers are large. Some people might shriek at the thought of being around so many family members, but I love it. I've always loved it.

Dad did have a blood clot and, because the doctor didn't want to give him blood thinning medication for fear it would cause his brain to bleed again, he had to go back to the hospital and have a stent put in. Mom wasn't very happy that we were ditching out on her again. She felt as if every time we were with her, something went wrong with Dad. The truth was, since November, everything was going wrong with Dad, and it wasn't only when we were with her. His body was slowly falling apart and new problems were continually being discovered.

I imagine she was right in feeling hurt, though. Since this began we had devoted every ounce of spare time to Dad and had rarely spent time with her. During one disagreement over the matter, I shouted, "You will have us the rest of our lives; every holiday, every function. We don't have the rest of our lives with Dad." It never occurred to me at the time that she really wouldn't have us the rest of our lives. One day we might be married or move away and she probably wouldn't get every holiday or function, but at the time it made for a righteous argument. One I thought would make her understand our feelings.

All I could think about, all that surged through my brain, was that Dad was dying, and time was the most valuable commodity I possessed. To me, she was being selfish and I was tired of it. Didn't she see how painful this was? Didn't she see that all we had left was limited time: one final Christmas, one final January 1st, one final February 1st? Every day was Dad's last day, unless God provided a miracle. This overrode any form of empathy I might have otherwise felt towards Mom. It kept me from seeing her frustration as a reaction to the fact that she just missed her children.

Dad was transported by ambulance back to the hospital in Lincoln. Angie traveled back to Cozad to grab an overnight bag along with other necessities, and we met her at the house to ride down together. Jakob was with us that weekend. As we pulled up to the hospital, he began to cry and refused to get out of the car. Everyone else went in to meet up with Dad while I waited, pleading with Jakob to go in.

But the hospital scared Jakob, and why wouldn't it? He was only four, and every time he went in there, Dad looked different. Doctors in white coats, resembling the villains in his cartoons, continually poked and prodded at Dad, undoubtedly helping him, but also causing visible pain. For all Jakob knew, the tubes and machines hooked onto Dad were more evidence they were turning him into the next Frankenstein.

I finally coaxed him out of the car, his tiny hand tucked inside of mine, his fingers white-knuckling my own. We stopped three times before we even made it to the entrance, as he littered the sidewalk with vomit. Each time, I rubbed his back and reassured him that everything was going to be okay: hiding my own doubts behind a comforting smile. Of course, I don't have the strongest stomach in the world either, so with each pit stop and whiff of partially digested juice and Cheetos, my comforting smile became an animated twitch between the gagging heaves. . . . And little Jakob just got more confused. I was pretty sure the pair of us might get admitted, ourselves, before we even made it to Dad's room. During the season of Dad's illness, in fact, Jakob vomited a lot. I almost vomited a lot. His poor little nerves just could not handle what was going on.

Dad wasn't in the hospital long. The surgery to place the stent was a quick scope through his groin, and he was able to come home within a few days.

After things settled down, we again discussed treatment options for the cancer. After seeing how sick chemotherapy and radiation had made Uncle Steve, it was natural that Dad refused it. Danny and I begged, however. We thought he was giving up hope and pressured him to get treatment. We had been told he had stage four cancer, the most advanced stage, but we couldn't imagine him going down without a fight. I sat at the foot of his La-Z-Boy recliner, pleading with him to reconsider. I was both relieved and guilt-ridden when he took out his marker board and scribbled "O.K."

I'd pressured him to go against what he initially wanted. He would do it for us. I felt so selfish. It was natural for me to want to hang on, but I knew his quality of life would decrease substantially, and the treatment would more than likely be ineffective. To me, prayers coupled with radiation treatments and chemotherapy just might work. I so badly wanted Dad to believe that as much as I did. Dad had faith and I knew he was praying, but I wondered if deep down he was certain of something we were not yet certain of: that he was dying.

I thought not doing anything meant that he, we, were giving up. I had always thought that way and it took a long time for me to realize that standing still, sitting still, and stopping doesn't always mean a person has given up or lost hope. We often fail to see acceptance as the beautiful response it is, and misinterpret it as giving up. Sometimes it's in stopping that hope is ignited. Many of us quote the first portion of the serenity prayer, "God, grant me the serenity to accept the things I cannot change, courage to change the things I can, and wisdom to know the difference," but are never able to respond to a situation, life change, or person with acceptance because we believe that nothing is out of our control. We foolishly believe there is nothing we cannot change.

The second part of the serenity prayer is much less familiar, and I believe even though it was obvious Dad was scared, he had come to it and we would all come to it:

> "Living one day at a time, enjoying one moment at a time. Accepting hardships as the pathway to peace. Taking, as He did, the sinful world as it is, not as I would have it. Trusting that He will make all things right if I surrender to His will. That I may be reasonably happy in this life and supremely happy with Him forever in the next. Amen."

Such beautiful words, but so difficult to live by. So many times I wish I would have more readily taken what was going on with Dad as Jesus takes this sinful world: "as it is." I was playing puppeteer with a father who could not speak or fully move on his own, pulling the strings in an effort to rewrite how his story might end.

Dad began chemotherapy and radiation not long after he agreed to it. It made him deathly sick. The smell of food made him vomit, his hair never grew back from when it was shaved before his surgery, and his weight dwindled from his inability to eat. His 5'7" build went from a sturdy, 185-pound, wood-cutting man to a fragile ninety pounds.

The feeding tube was still in his abdomen, but once he'd gained full swallowing functionality back, we stopped using it and capped it. Eventually Dad made the decision to remove the feeding tube, so it couldn't be used merely to keep him alive longer if it came down to that. His scream thundered through the doctor's office the day they yanked it out of his abdomen. I thought him so brave and courageous. Danny and I didn't beg him otherwise this time. We loved him too much to keep him with us if the only thing sustaining him was nutrients being fed through a tube.

Our small community rallied around our family, just like it had a couple of years before for Uncle Steve. With the help of life-long friends from Dad's work, Monroe Automotive, a fundraiser was held that raised enough money for our family to pay off thousands of dollars of medical expenses, as well as the costs of the chemotherapy and radiation treatments. Friends graciously delivered meals and words of encouragement, day after day. I believed God was providing for us through the generosity of others as he spoke to my heart:

> So do not worry saying, "What shall we eat?" or "What shall we drink?" or "What shall we wear?" For the pagans run after all these things, and your heavenly Father knows that you need them. But seek first His kingdom and His righteousness, and all these things will be given to you as well.
> – Matthew 6:31–33

Dad was getting visibly worse, and each day seemed like an uphill battle. He was like a forty-year-old in a seventy-year-old's body, no longer the sturdily built father whose shoulders I rode on as a child. Now he could barely shoulder his own weight.

By the end of the chemotherapy and radiation, the tumors had all grown. Not one had shrunk. Dad was put on hospice care shortly after that, given at most six months to live. We were supposed to accept that his death was inevitable and were given books, from the social worker in charge of his case, containing information on losing loved ones and the grieving process. Those who are aware of the stages of grief know that after the initial shock and denial comes pain and guilt, then anger, bargaining, depression, and finally acceptance. I hit every stage.

Dad turned forty-three on the 26th of April, and I remember thinking, "He's done it! He's made it past forty-two: there's hope yet." I completed my college finals the first week of May and moved back home immediately. I still worked Monday through Friday in Kearney, but it was only a forty-five-minute drive each way, and I knew every minute I had with Dad was precious.

By May his eyes were sunken, his skin was clammy to the touch, and the smell of death engulfed him. I'd smelt that smell before. It's the smell of life leaving the body, of organs shutting down. It's not rancid or unbearable, just distinct. No words can adequately describe it, let alone describe the piercing feeling it brings. It's like an invisible fog, so thick you can feel it wrap around your body and begin crushing your heart.

One morning after I'd moved back home, I awoke to commotion in Dad's room. I ran in, hair disheveled and glasses on, to see Grandma Rose and Angie holding Dad's arms as his whole body convulsed and his teeth chattered together. The whites of his eyes, now a yellow hue, rolled into the back of his head as he shook uncontrollably. I stared.

CHAPTER TWO

Amazing Grace

I WAS FROZEN.

I watched as Dad slowly stopped jerking and his body relaxed. I looked into his eyes. There he was. As I exhaled a sigh of relief, I realized I was grateful for the seizure; which horrified me more than the seizure itself. I wondered what had become of me. Was I so terrified of losing Dad that I'd rather have him suffering beside me than restored and away from me? Would I rather watch his body violently seize than have to witness his dying moment? Yes.

We all took turns in the worn, wooden chair at Dad's bedside; Angie and I often with Bibles in our lap, reading to Dad. I read the book of Revelation aloud, intentionally describing the New Jerusalem. In my mind, Heaven was similar. As much as I needed Dad to have a vivid image, a mental photograph to cling to, I needed it as well. He listened as I described a city made of pure gold, as pure as glass, and opaque walls built with jasper. Foundations of amethysts, emeralds, rubies, and sapphires would replace the brick and mortar foundations he was used to. No need for a sun or moon in this city, in this unfathomable place, as the illumination of God's glory was enough. Flashing fluorescent lights and sixty-watt light bulbs were obsolete.

As I read about the river flowing from the throne, I noticed Dad had reached over and was twirling his finger in the glass of water on his bedside stand. He was already there. Streaming his fingers through those crystal cool waters; in the river of the water of life, he'd approach death no more.

There were many times I thought that Dad experienced glimpses of heaven or heavenly hosts. He'd calmly and peacefully lift his arm and point towards the corner of the room. We'd follow his gaze, but there was nothing our eyes could see. Critics might say it was the morphine: that Dad was experiencing hallucinations. I believe as Dad approached death, he inched closer and closer to God, and God inched closer and closer to Him.

Dad would recline in his La-Z-Boy, in the living room, on days he felt well. Other days, he stayed in bed. We would try to sit with him while he was awake. Sometimes, however, we just couldn't be in there the whole time, even taking turns. Grandma brought a small, gold-colored bell from her house so Dad could ring it if he needed something when we weren't in the room.

"Ding, ding, ding"; it would echo through the house and we'd rush to Dad's side. He'd point to his water mug. We'd get water for him, set the mug on his bedside stand and then leave the room. The bell would ring again; Dad would be holding a piece of ice shaking his head left to right to indicate "no." We would take the water, refill it with no ice, bring it back and once again leave the room. "Ding, ding, ding. . . . Ding. Ding. Ding."

Sometimes Dad wanted ice, sometimes he didn't. Sometimes he wanted pain medicine or his pillow fluffed. He seemed to want more things when we were out of the room than when we were in it. He could run us ragged, so it was best just to sit with Dad if he was awake. Dad was sly; I don't think he wanted to be alone, but I also think, for the first time, he had us women at his beck and call, and he secretly loved it. I still laugh out loud today when I think of Dad dinging that bell. As annoying as it was, it was worse when it stopped ringing.

Danny, Jakob, and I were called into Dad's room one day, close to the end. Dad presented us with gifts that Angie had helped pick out. Danny and Jakob each got a gold cross necklace. My gift was a red and gold coated rose: coated so I would forever have a rose from Dad, one that would never wilt or die. Dad always sent me flowers for Valentine's Day or for my birthday. I guess it was his way of saying I would always have flowers from him even if he wasn't there to send them. But I didn't want one rose from him that would last forever. I just wanted him to last forever.

On another afternoon, Danny came into Dad's room with his acoustic guitar. In the six months that Dad had been sick, Danny had taught himself how to play. He would sit by Dad's bed performing the newest songs he'd learned. Dad watched with such a deep sense of sadness and concern. He worried about Danny: whether or not he'd be okay after Dad was gone. Each time Danny's guitar pick brought those six strings to life, Dad's worry would begin to dissipate; his head would fall gently onto his pillow and his eyes would close. That day, Danny played "Amazing Grace." As he struck the first chords, Dad began to sing out. He wasn't singing with words, like you and I would, and it was as if he didn't know. He still couldn't speak, but at the top of his voice, his murmurs rang out to the tune, "Amazing grace, how sweet the sound that saved a wretch like me; I once was lost, but now am found, was blind, but now I see." Tears fell from my eyes. Tears fell from Danny's eyes. Tears fell from all our eyes. When words fail, music speaks.

Not many days after Dad sang out, he slipped into a coma. A deep unconsciousness washed over his body as his eyes stared blankly at the wall. I desperately wanted him to come back to me. I wanted the relief that followed from Dad coming to from his seizures. I wanted to look into his eyes and say "there you are." But he wasn't there. Dad was no longer Dad.

The bell no longer rang, and we no longer left his side. The nurse came that morning and took his vitals; she pressed her stethoscope to his heart, wrapped the blood pressure cuff around his arm, and said his blood pressure was very low. She advanced her stethoscope to his abdomen; his bowels were shutting down. We were told it was probable he would not live to see the next day. She advised us to say our goodbyes, even if we felt he wouldn't hear us.

We all took turns going into Dad's room alone. When it was my turn, I told him everything I could think of, even trying to reply to the things I imagined he would tell me.

"Dad, I'm going to be okay. I'm going to miss you so much, but I'll be okay."

"I will look out for Danny and Jakob."

"Danny will be okay, don't you worry."

"I love you so much!"

"I'm gonna see you again one day. It's going to feel like forever to me, but it won't for you."

"I'll never, never forget you."

As I blurted out everything I could think of I asked God, "God, why can't I hear my dad's voice? Why can't I hear him call me 'Pumpkin' one more time, and hear him tell me everything will be okay? Why can't I just have a conversation with him? I want to know what he wants to tell me." My heart's cry was, "Why can't I just have that?"

God whispered back to my heart, "My child, you may not hear your earthly father's voice anymore, but you are beginning to hear mine."

I will never leave you nor forsake you.

– Joshua 1:5

After everyone had poured their hearts out to Dad, I sat by his bedside holding his hand. His hands were wrinkled, wrinkled much beyond his four decades, and his fingers were so skinny that their coldness drew the warmth out of mine. Grandma, Angie, my best friend and cousin, Jenna, and I sat and waited. For fear he might slip away and I not be there, I glued myself to the chair, afraid to even use the bathroom.

His breathing entranced us all. No longer the automated sound of a ventilator, it was a rattling, shallow inhale and exhale—the sound of last breaths. His chest rose . . . paused . . . fell. Each breath he took, I prayed he would take another. The pause between his breaths lengthened until the pause remained.

I dropped off the wooden chair to my knees beside the hospital bed as goosebumps shot down my entire body. "God, please take him now. Just wrap your arms around him and take him home," I prayed. All of us had sat so quietly listening to the sound of his raspy breathing that when it stopped there was no sound at all. I stared at him. I'd never seen anyone die before. I didn't cry. I just stared.

As soon as I realized the words I had just prayed, I wanted to take them back! I wanted to hit the rewind button on life; I would relive the agony of his illness to his death a thousand times over if it meant he could come back.

Dad had barely left us, and I was already scrambling.

We sat there with Dad's body for nearly an hour. The boys, who had left that morning to go bridge jumping, were called home. I had screamed at Danny when they left: "You are so stupid and so selfish, leaving home fully aware of what the nurse said! Not only that, but for going bridge jumping when you could get impaled by something near the bridge and die yourself!"

My brother and step-brothers would drive to a nearby lake and identify all of the places where a bridge crossed over the water.

The higher the bridge, the better. They would then jump over the edge of the bridge and into the water, seeing who could do the craziest tricks. In rural Nebraska, a lot of these bridges were old wooden bridges and had left-over debris beneath them from years of wear and tear or the repair of the bridge. This debris was often hidden beneath the water's surface, so it was only a guess if there were or were not any harmful items hidden from view. It was also a guess as to how deep the water beneath the bridge was, and if it was deep enough to sustain a high jump without slamming into the bottom of the lake. Hence the adrenaline rush! I'd heard a story about a boy who jumped off a bridge and into the water; he didn't jump far enough out from the bridge, however, and got impaled by an old wooden pole that was hidden just beneath the water's surface. Dad had told me that story. I don't know if it was true or not, but it was enough to keep me from ever going bridge-jumping. And it was also enough to keep me from wanting my brothers to bridge-jump!

As Danny had walked away from me that morning to go do the very thing I feared would steal him from me too, my voice reached a crescendo. "You are going to regret this for the rest of your life!!!" I screamed out of my own pain.

Danny had screamed back at me, "I cannot sit around and watch him die, Holly!"

Danny loved Dad more than he loved anyone. Dad knew this, and he was more concerned about Danny than he was about anyone else.

Danny couldn't believe that Dad was gone, and as he walked into Dad's room, his heart broke within him. I knew that Danny wished he had stayed, and for one of the first times in my life I didn't say to my younger brother, "Told ya so."

Eventually, the mortician came and took Dad's body. Just like that, both his body and soul were gone. Not long after, the medical company from whom we'd rented the hospital bed came and removed that as well. Piece by piece, I watched the remnants of Dad's last months of life disappear in a matter of hours.

The one thing a grieving person wants more than having their loved one back is for time to stand still. Though our world stops, and life stands still for us, everyone and everything else keeps moving. I walked, lifelessly, outside to the back of our house and sat behind the shed. Staring into the sky, I tried to process that this was really happening. No pinch or great jolt was going to wake me from a dream; this was my nightmarish reality.

Dad had built this shed when I was little. It was a small, stand-alone building a few feet from our house. Dad's hands had created its miniature, house-like shape, laid its asphalt shingles, and painted its wooden boards a milky white. But the white no longer shone as bright, and chips of paint and wood lay scattered along the ground beside it.

I used to climb to the top of this shed when I was a little girl, sit on the roof, stare at the sky, and dream that I was a princess trapped in a tower. I'd first have to climb on top of the doghouse, which sat right up against the shed, then jump my hardest and use all my strength to pull myself up onto the roof. I was a gymnast though, so this wasn't anything out of the ordinary for me. Sometimes I'd sit up there for hours, daydreaming and creating stories in my head. Whenever I'd get caught, Dad would tell me to get down immediately because, he said, I would get hurt. I would have rather fallen off the shed that day and experienced the physical pain from a fall instead of the emotional pain I was feeling inside. I no longer felt like a princess trapped in a tower, but like a street beggar trapped in a reality I wanted desperately to escape.

I kept begging God to turn back time, to give Dad back to me. All of the "he's not going to be there" thoughts flooded into my mind. He wouldn't be at my college graduation, he wouldn't walk me down the aisle at my wedding, and he wouldn't be there to hold my babies. He would never be at anything again.

I knew that in a matter of days, after the funeral, other people would expect me to move on. I didn't want to move forward. It was then my first tears began to fall. I wanted to scream, to hurl all the hurt I was feeling at God and turn my back, leaving Him to stand alone in the puddle of my tears and in the pit of my agony.

Grandma Rose and Angie planned most of Dad's funeral service, while I had an addition of my own, at my dad's request. Prior to his death, I had written a poem from Dad's perspective and read it to him; he thought it belonged in his funeral program. When the time came, I dropped it off at the funeral home to be added to Dad's service. One last time, Dad would be given his voice as friends, family, and co-workers piled into the pews at the service, opened the program, and read:

I closed my eyes and I am whole.
Breathed deep and I was healed.
I'll only blink and you'll be here.
Where I am, there is no time—
no time to cry, no time to regret.

Just close your eyes and you'll see me—
my smile, familiar strut.
Breathe deep and you'll remember—
the smell of my cologne as I walked by,
the grease on my work boots.
For you there's time—
time to heal, but don't regret.

When you need me most, I'll be near.
Just close your eyes . . .

I heard people whispering at the funeral, "He looks terrible." As they peered into the casket at Dad's painted face and sunken skin, they thought my dad looked ugly. Terrible. I'm sure that's not what they meant, but that's what I heard. I don't think I was even supposed to hear that much, but I've got good ears and a keen eye. I often get called nosey and am eyeballed with the "what are you staring at: do you want me to jump you?" look, but the fact of the matter is, I enjoy observing and studying people. I should have been an anthropologist: at least then I'd have an excuse.

Of course Dad looked terrible. Cancer had depleted him, in a matter of six months, from a walking, breathing, stocky man in his forties to a sickly, ashen-hued man appearing to be in his seventies, now stiff in a casket. Everything about that is terrible . . . was terrible.

Natalie Grant's song "Held" echoed through the Lutheran church where we held Dad's funeral ceremony; it bounced off the reds and yellows of the stained glass windows. It was a song we'd chosen for the ceremony. As I sat in the front pew, Dad's casket before me and flower arrangements surrounding me, tears streamed down my face as it played:

To think that Providence
would take a child from his mother
while she prays, is appalling.
Who told us we'd be rescued?
What has changed and
why should we be saved from nightmares?
We're asking why this happens to us
who have died to live, it's unfair.
This is what it means to be held;
How it feels, when the sacred is torn from your life
and you survive.
This is what it is to be loved and to know

that the promise was that when everything fell
we'd be held.
This hand is bitterness;
we want to taste it and
let the hatred numb our sorrows.
The wise hand opens slowly
to lilies of the valley and tomorrow;
this is what it means to be held.

CHAPTER THREE

Unsettled

I TREMBLED.

The railroad tracks were situated a block from our house. Like the graffitied train cars, tattooed in neon bubble letters, that shook through our quiet town each day and disappeared out of sight, Dad's funeral also shook us up and then ended. The meat and mozzarella-layered lasagnas, pre-baked casseroles, and buttermilk brownies stopped being delivered to the house, and we were back to bologna sandwiches.

The dark Nebraska dirt had been packed on top of Dad's grave, as if life had dusted her hands at a finished task and said, "It's over. Move on." I wasn't trying to be morbid, but I wondered what Dad looked like as a week passed, two weeks passed; how long did it take a body to decay? How long would it take for this daddy of mine, who helped form me from nothing, to become nothing? Nothing more than bones.

Dad's clothes hung in his closet. His steel-toed work boots, which previously stood by the door on the white, linoleum floor in our kitchen, were tucked neatly away. I wanted them back by the door, but there was no man to fill them. Some man, somewhere, would wake up at 5 a.m., brew Folger's coffee, slip on his work boots, start up his truck and head off to work, but that man was not my dad. My dad was gone.

I carefully breathed in the remaining scent on Dad's navy blue Nike sweatshirt and tucked it into my bag. We'd be getting rid of most of his stuff, as there'd be no place left to keep it. We would lose the home I grew up in, as the bank prepared to foreclose due to unpayable house payments. Life would never be the same again.

There's a large construction company in my hometown that does jobs all over the state: its headquarters sit on the same highway we lived just a block from. I used to watch the huge red and white trucks pour the wet mixture when they were resurfacing the local sidewalks and parking lots. A day or two later, I'd pass by the worksite to see the cement fully hardened, no longer shiftable. Somberness poured over me like the cement I'd watched being dumped from those trucks, threatening to harden me into a state of grief. The permanence and heaviness of that cement as it set resembled the deep sadness embedding inside my heart; I wasn't sure I'd ever break free from it. May dragged on into August, like a boat anchor pulling along a lakebed. The fall semester of college approached, and heaps of books entombed me.

My sleep was haunted by visions of Dad's dead body, and my own screaming would often startle me awake. In an attempt to suffocate the nightmares, I would bury my tear-streaked face into my pillow with such ferocity that it often felt like I, in turn, was suffocating. The dreams were lifelike. A gaping cut from surgery would split the side of Dad's head and I'd be told he was dying all over again. I'd have to load his dead body into a hearse, his rubbery skin pressed against mine, the smell of formaldehyde choking me. As darkness fell, the horrors continued.

When beams of morning light burst through my bedroom window, I would tuck the duvet high up on my chest and shut the alarm clock off. Pulling my body out of bed was like pulling an adhesive strip off a wall. I missed so many classes between August and December it's a wonder I even passed. Many days, I'd only make it to work—and then only because I needed the money.

I lived off-campus, but I ventured back to the residence halls once a week on Wednesday night for Bible study. I couldn't open my Bible without crying, though. My vulnerability was as thin as a sheet of tissue paper: the slightest ruffling—and I tore. There I was, laid bare before God, and I didn't know how to handle it. Time and time again, a crusty scab was ripped off my heart, causing fresh blood to seep to the surface. My raw wound oozed and throbbed with gut-wrenching agony. The girls in my Bible study were encouraging and sympathetic, but I couldn't be honest about the depths of my pain.

I may have asked for prayer a couple of times, but not often enough. I knew I wasn't the same, but I feared being labeled. Being labeled weak. Being labeled a sinner. Fearing that I wouldn't be considered resilient. Because this was a Christian circle, in my mind I thought I had to portray myself as a hopeful and holy girl: always positive, always trusting God. No one ever told me that's what was expected and, looking back, I don't believe that it was, but for some reason I just felt like I couldn't be authentic. I felt that I couldn't utter the words that were encased in the back of my throat and groaning to come out:

"God feels pretty far from me right now."

"I can't get out of bed."

"God hurt me. Whether it was in His absence or in His sovereignty, He hurt me."

I was afraid that at my first words of confession, the other girls would immediately encourage me to talk to a pastor or a Christian counselor.

We sometimes do that as Christians: quickly pass the buck of comforting and healing on to someone else "more qualified," because we don't recognize Jesus's power in us. In us Bible study attendees: sinners made new, untitled Christians. Sometimes people do need to be referred to someone else—other times they just need the hand nearest them to reach out and transfer Jesus. Buried in the ocean depths of my soul was a whisper crying out, "Jesus, I need you," but the voice burying that, the one that cried louder said, "Jesus, I don't deserve you."

My subtly curved smile and camouflaged eyes were a false front, like those old-fashioned building fronts one learns about in history class, the ones that made a building look larger than it really was. They portrayed something that wasn't truly as it appeared. I didn't know how to live in this new life I'd inherited along with Dad's life insurance pay-out. I didn't know how to be the girl without a dad, to be the girl who cried when the lights went out, to be the girl who dreamt of dead bodies and who didn't want to face the day. My cousins would understand, because they had been through this with their Dad. Jenna, the one closest to my age, would definitely understand, but talking to them would make me cry too much. I knew I would break down, and I so desperately wanted to be strong. Grandma Rose would understand; she'd buried her husband and both of her sons . . . just like Naomi in the book of Ruth. But I didn't want to make Grandma cry.

I didn't want to be the girl who couldn't cope. My own fears kept me isolated; my own pride kept me retreating deeper and deeper, because I cared too much about what people would think of me. That's a dangerous place to be.

Wednesday nights I went to Bible study; Friday and Saturday nights I partied. I didn't turn twenty-one until January of that year, so I couldn't go to the bars, but that didn't matter because my friends and I knew people who bought us alcohol. With a beer bong held high above our heads, we'd compete to see who could finish it the fastest. As the cheapest can of beer was poured down a red funnel, which filtered through a rubber tube jammed down our throats, we hooted and hollered like contenders in an Olympic sport. As we held this beer bong above our heads, God simultaneously hung something else above me. He simultaneously hangs something of more worth over each of us, in moments just like these, and in the now. But I didn't see it. Sometimes we still don't see it.

I see it now.

> His banner over me is love.
>
> – Song of Solomon 2:4

You can call me a hypocrite: I called myself a hypocrite. It was as if I thought the double life could save me. If one way wouldn't heal the pain, the other could kill it. But mixing alcohol and grief is a toxic concoction whose potency burns the entire way down. It didn't heal nor did it kill—more like just temporarily stunned. The day following a drunken binge, guilt and shame would come knocking on the door of my heart. I'd have to entertain grief along with the two of them (all while being hung over). I was miserable.

I thought if I found love, found "The One," things would get better. The sting of delayed rejection only added to the festering wound inside my heart, though. I say "delayed" because when you're drunk and interacting with drunken men, the rejection isn't always immediate.

On Sunday mornings I'd make sure to attend church. Yeah; I know.

Too lazy to dig through my clothes for my Sunday best, I'd throw my clothes from Saturday night back on. They'd go into the dryer with a Snuggle dryer sheet for a quick dry, then I'd tug them on, pour coffee into my mug, and drag myself blurry-eyed into church—sometimes still smelling like smoke and left-over alcohol from the night before. I was desperate. I wanted to be happy again. I wanted to love life and be excited by life. I wanted someone to love me. I wanted to love someone. I wanted a father. I didn't want to be the girl I was.

Tears streamed down my face as I sobbed alone in my room. These weren't subtly flowing tears. I'm not talking about nagging dripping-faucet kind of tears, but thunderous Niagara Falls kind of tears: tears that rush down with no apparent end in sight. No matter how much you try, those tears won't stop. Red-puffy-eyes-associated-with-constant-nose-running kind of tears. Lamenting with choppy breathing, hyperventilation, and stuttering. I cried these tears. You've been there too, I know, although maybe for different reasons.

Attempting to infuse myself with inspiration and the ever sought-after happiness, I sticky-tacked motivational quotes and Bible verses all over the door and walls in my room. Nothing helped. Darkness threw its mourning veil over my heart and depression chased me like a midday shadow.

Shortly before Christmas that year, I fell back into a relationship with my high school boyfriend. We had been on-again-off-again since I was fourteen and now, at the age of twenty, it seemed the only place to go. As I clung to him, I was clinging to the life I once had; and now at least I had motivation to get out of bed in the mornings. I thought God had answered my prayers and I could live the life I wanted, happily ever after.

My high school beau wore Wrangler jeans and plaid button-up shirts every day of the week. A pinch of Copenhagen chewing tobacco typically bulged from the corner of his bottom lip, giving him a rough and tough appearance. He plowed fields, rode horses, castrated bulls; he was a cowboy kind of guy. His straight red hair resembled the shade of rust on metal, inspiring the kids in high school to nickname him "Rusty."

I was still a mess, despite our relationship coming together again. There was no length I wouldn't go for attention or to make a point. We both often hurt each other deeply, as we always had. One afternoon, I jumped out of his moving (not too terribly fast) flat-bed pickup truck onto a gravel road. We were arguing and I wanted to get away (apparently, pretty badly). I can't remember if it was the look in his eyes or the words that rolled off his tongue, but the rocks embedded deep in the palms of my hands echoed it too: "You're crazy!" I was a bit psycho at the time. (If you have done something similar, I won't apologize for saying it's psycho. Take comfort in the fact that we're all crazy humans at times, but if we believe in Jesus then we're on the road to being made more like Him—even if it takes getting beat up by gravel while on that road.)

In my heart, I knew something was missing. My boyfriend wasn't who I needed and I wasn't who he needed. For a Christmas present that year, he gave me a Bath & Body Works basket filled with shower gel, lotion, and body spray, all of which were coconut scented. I hate coconut—the taste, the texture, the smell. Although we had only barely begun dating again, I was crushed that after seven years of on and off dating he didn't know this about me. I was grateful for the gift, but this seemingly silly hurt only reiterated the feeling in my being that something was missing.

This time around, the high school beau and I made it about nine months before our relationship shattered. He broke up with me. I was always getting broken up with, and not just by him. You'd think I'd be used to it or get the hint, but it wasn't any easier this time. My heart imploded, caving in on itself and trapping shards of rejection inside. It felt as though everyone was leaving me and nobody wanted me. The feeling of rejection I had felt as a six-year-old little girl hit even deeper and harder; neither Barbie nor a twenty dollar bill could chase it away any longer.

My guy had a good heart, but I wasn't good for him and he wasn't good for me. He used to sing to me the lyrics of Diamond Rio's song "What Might Have Been": *"I try not to think about what might have been,"* his alto voice would belt, *"'cause that was then, and we have taken different roads."* We had most definitely taken different roads. Somewhere along the line I had veered onto a side path, and our hopes and dreams no longer aligned. His cowboy boots kicked up gravel as they walked the familiar country roads of my hometown. My high-heeled shoes clicked together as I walked my own yellow-brick road to some far-off Oz.

I had been gathering the pieces of my old life, trying to fit them back together again. God didn't want that. He wanted to start sculpting something different. None of my attempts at piecing my life together had been His vision. None of my attempts at love had been His God-written love story, because I was trying to change characters I didn't have the power to change. My attempts were the best I could create for myself, because they were all I knew. But they weren't God's best; they were not all that He knew.

God lifted my mourning veil as a father lifts his daughter's bridal veil before handing her to her groom. He removed the black polyester netting and set a white veil in its place, kissed my cheek, and placed my hand in Jesus's hand. "Here is my Son," He said. "I don't have to tell Him to take care of you. It's the very nature of His being."

In the heat of the summer of 2007, I was once again alone, but I wasn't lonely. Daylight is longer during the summer; the strength of the sun fights off the darkness well into the evening. It was symbolic of what was happening in my heart. Nightmares no longer haunted my sleep, although holes and cracks covered my soul, like a wall where too many pictures once hung. I was broken, but it was those cracks, those holes, that allowed God's light to filter in.

> *"Ring the bells that still can ring*
> *Forget your perfect offering*
> *There is a crack in everything*
> *That's how the light gets in."*
>   – Leonard Cohen

> "I am the light of the world. Whoever follows me will never walk in darkness, but will have the light of life."
>   – John 8:12

I was wounded, as you've no doubt been wounded. I processed the hurt and the pain. Each reflection brought its own fresh sores. God handed me a cup of healing, one I could partake of because Jesus chose to hold onto his cup in the garden of Gethsemane. I could drink in its sweetness, let it enter my bloodstream and be carried throughout my body. The world handed me a different cup: a cup filled to the brim with bitterness. I could swallow its poison—and turn into a God-hater, a man-hater, and a life-hater. I could easily adopt the woe-is-me mentality and feel sorry for myself and my pain. But I wanted something more.

Line by line I read the Scriptures. My eyes met the words; they came alive as if they'd laid dormant, waiting for me. I began to understand that God didn't take my dad because I was being punished or because He loved me less—it was just one of those unfortunate events. The reality of life is that some people have it tougher than others; some experience more hurt and more pain. I don't believe it's because they're unlucky or cursed. I don't believe I'm unlucky or cursed. I can't pretend to know why things happen. I can come up with all sorts of opinions in my state of grief, but actually that's all they are, opinions. They're also most likely heavily biased due to my emotional state.

The *whys* are there; they'll always be there, trying to wrap our hearts up in an endless knot. Attempting to get us stuck on a question whose answer, even if we receive it, doesn't alleviate our pain. I wanted God to hurt for causing me hurt. I wanted him to feel like He messed up. But I believe that God was hurt before I intentionally tried to hurt him. He hurt because I hurt. He didn't make a mistake. If our home is in heaven and that's where we belong, where our souls long to be even if we don't tune into our spiritual longings, then all God had done was to call Dad out of the foreign land of this world and back to his home country.

I began to understand that the men who had hurt my feelings weren't evil or bad, though some had done what I considered bad things. They were like me: broken individuals trying to fit into and live out a life in a broken world. They made mistakes like I did and hurt like I did. When God begins changing your perspective, when He begins renewing your mind and allowing you to think and see like Him, it doesn't always come easily. Sometimes it's difficult for this new godly perspective, this new heavenly frame of reference, to be the place we operate from, to be the place we see and make decisions from. I didn't make excuses for the hurt caused me, nor did I make excuses for what I did. God simply began to challenge me not to judge the people in my past, nor my own past self. Even my psycho behavior did not mean I was a crazy and unlovable person. God is a good God, and He works all things for the good of those who love him (Romans 8: 28).

I had to accept this difficult path my life had taken, learn from it, and keep moving forward. I needed Father God. I knew how to be a child; I knew how to throw tantrums; but I didn't know how to be an adult, how to maturely love, maturely give, maturely receive. I needed a father's advice and fatherly words of instruction, words of wisdom. I needed a strong hand and a stern hand—a hand of guidance. I didn't have my earthly father—and that made me recognize my Heavenly Father, cry out for my Heavenly Father.

I needed Jesus, the Lover of my soul. I began to understand what it meant to be the bride of Christ, to understand that God loves each of us as if there is only one of us. His love for me is relentless; He loves me more than anyone on this earth ever could. When no one else wanted me, not only did He want me, He <u>fought</u> for me. He fights for all of us. And once He has us, He doesn't neglect us or toss us aside, but He rejoices over us; He adores us.

> "As a bridegroom rejoices over his bride, so will your God rejoice over you."
>
> – Isaiah 62:5

This love of Christ that comforts grief, heals broken hearts, and restores identities was right before me, right upon me. But until it ravished my soul, I didn't know I needed it so desperately. Though summer break was again coming to a close, mountainous heaps of books didn't threaten to entomb me now; not because there were few books, but because I was walking with God. This Christ, this God, purposed to resurrect me, no matter my circumstances.

School began with the buzz of college students making their way back on campus and with me actually attending all of my classes. I spent a lot of time focusing on school work and anticipating graduation day—even though I would continue on through the summer and through another year for graduate school.

Not long after the fall semester began, a young man walked into my life. Actually, he walked into nearly every classroom I did; we were both business and accounting majors and so had most of the same classes. At roughly six feet two inches tall, he towered above my five foot frame. His strong build, dark hair, and dark eyes thrust him into the actor Pierce Brosnan's look-alike category. Up until then, I had viewed him as a nerdy and arrogant, compare-exam-scores-with-other-top-students kind of guy. But like the shifting of the ocean tides, my opinion was changing.

The eagerness with which he shot his hand up in the air to answer a question no longer seemed nerdy, but intriguing. (Did he really know all the answers? Was he really that intelligent?) His repeated 90 percent and above exam scores no longer spoke of an obvious lack of a social life, but of consistency and focus. That he sat in the front row of every classroom no longer meant he was a teacher's pet, but someone who paid appropriate attention.

I began to spend a bit more time poofing my hair each morning (this was when the front-bang poof, secured by bobby pins and extra-hold hairspray, was in style). A spritz of perfume became an everyday accessory. As I subtly began verbalizing my availability, a mutual interest developed.

I prayed about a relationship with him beforehand, and I felt as if God was asking me to be still. I did try to remain still (I really did), but the butterflies in my stomach burst forth and I couldn't help but take flight along with them. We began dating. This college beau and I discussed faith and God; there were obvious differences in what we both believed, but we built our relationship on mutual respect for one another. We never fought; I did my absolute best to hide that emotionally needy side of myself. I was determined to be the world's perfect girlfriend.

College beau taught me how to waltz, took me ice skating, complimented me, and showed genuine interest and intrigue in who I was. He helped me with my homework (bonus!), and he arrived at each of our classes before me in order to leave a sticky note with a special message underneath my desk. I was infatuated; I thought he was The One.

One particular evening, we sat discussing life and asking random, "would-you-ever" questions, when we happened upon the topic of race. "Would you ever date a black woman?" I asked. He replied by saying he had no prejudices, but didn't think he would. I agreed I probably wouldn't date a black man either; both of us thinking there would be obvious cultural differences. Midwestern Nebraska isn't the most cosmopolitan place in the world, so we both assumed the chances of meeting and falling in love with an African-American were slim. I'm certain God, in his omniscience, was shaking his head, saying, "You have no idea what I have planned for you," and I didn't.

In November that year, with the crunchy fall leaves carpeting the ground and winter's frost fast approaching, I sat sipping vanilla bean flavored coffee and reading my Bible. (Yes, I still read my Bible, even though I'd disobeyed God's "be still" prompting.) The country of India somehow entered my mind; instantly my heartbeat began to rise from a soft patter to a brisk flutter. I hadn't thought about India for a long time.

The movie *A Little Princess*, adapted from Frances Hodgson Burnett's 1905 children's novel, had captured my heart and imagination as a child. When ten-year-old Sara's father receives orders to leave his station in India to fight overseas, Sara and her father board a boat to New York. When the boat docks in New York, Sara's father enrolls her in a boarding school and bids her a tearful farewell. Sara's imagination and tales of India gain her popularity among her classmates, as they live each adventure vicariously through her stories.

Not long after her arrival, the stern headmistress, whom Sara is already in conflict with, receives word that Sara's father is dead, which means no more money to pay for her school tuition. To keep from being tossed on the street amidst the other orphans and beggars, Sara becomes a servant of the boarding school, mopping the floors and cleaning up after her previous classmates. Despite difficulties and moments of unbelief, she uses the power of her imagination and her own belief that she is still a princess to keep hope alive.

As a little girl, the line in the movie in which Sara says, "I am a princess. All girls are. Even if they live in tiny old attics. Even if they dress in rags; even if they aren't pretty, or smart, or young. They're still princesses. All of us." kept me believing I really was a princess. I only wish I had known these words from God's lips and heard His soft voice, as He does whisper this to every little girl and every young woman—to every woman. "You are a princess! Whether you live in a tiny old attic. Whether you dress in rags, and even if you don't see yourself as pretty or smart or young. You're still a princess!" Movie lines fade, quotes are forgotten, but God's words, spoken to us, remain active and alive. They are an unshakable foundation, if we build with them. The world's brick and mortar words are merely debris in the aftermath of disaster.

Sara's riches-to-rags story continued, but the point is it was those very tales of India, told by a child in a movie, which planted a desire in my heart to experience that country for myself. Nearly fifteen years later the dream remained: drastically transformed from a child's desire of witnessing princesses, exotic gardens, and far-off places to sharing the gospel and a message of hope with an impoverished people. God transformed my desire from an ambitious yearning defined by my childhood to one defined by His heart. He planted the desire within me, and then molded into His vision the child-like vision I'd created.

Unsure where to begin with this renewed passion for India, I visited the website of the organization with which I had previously gone on a two-week mission trip to Lima, Peru. As I browsed through their upcoming trips, I found one scheduled to India in the month of July. I sat down at the desk in my auditing class the next morning to find a sticky note underneath which read *"India awaits you"*—and it did. I immediately applied, was accepted, and began raising funds to go. College beau was incredibly supportive and donated money towards my trip, as did my high school beau (a surprisingly large amount), along with many others. God used individuals I didn't even imagine He would use to help get me there.

Anyone who has raised funds for a mission trip or who is a full-time missionary knows how difficult it is to ask friends, family, co-workers—basically everyone you know and everyone the people you know, know—for money. I've always dreaded this part of missions; however, God, my friends, my family, and my co-workers have always proved faithful. If not for their support, I would not have been able to go. Over the next few months, the funds poured in. Not only did the funds pour in from people, but God used an unusual event to get me to the total sum I needed: $4,000.

By this time it was May 2008, about a week before my college finals. I had just finished one of my classes and was driving from the university back to my apartment with a full white chocolate mocha in my cup-holder and Christian radio blasting from the speakers. As the traffic light ahead turned red and I began to slow to a stop, a Jimmy John's delivery car slammed into the back of mine, causing my coffee to erupt out of its cup and onto the ceiling of my car. This rocket-launch-hit propelled my car into the car ahead of me, which then slammed that car into the car ahead of it.

At first, I wasn't sure if I was more upset about losing my mocha or that my car might be totaled. As we all began piling out of our cars to inspect the damage, the kid who had hit me from behind admitted he switched lanes quickly and was not paying attention to the stopping traffic. After the police came and everything got sorted out, I and the two others who were hit were told to get an estimate of the damage that was done to our cars, turn it into the delivery kid's insurance company, and wait for a claim to pay for the damage.

My car was still driveable and, thankfully, no one was hurt. The next day, I took my car into the body shop to get it looked over; I left with an estimate of damage nearing $3,500. A few weeks later, an insurance adjuster came to look at my car, to investigate whether or not the claim was reasonable. Shortly thereafter, I received a check for nearly $3,500. Then, not too long after the check arrived, a mechanic friend offered to fix my car for substantially less, which gave me an additional $1,500 to put toward my mission trip . . . which was exactly the amount I needed to make it to the required $4,000.

Having a car accident while I was a sleep-deprived student in the middle of final exam week was not my idea of a good thing. Losing a $5 specialty coffee meant to combat that sleep-deprivation was also not my idea of a good thing. However, God used that accident to provide the remainder of my funds towards my trip to India, as well as to teach me that He is always faithful and He always provides. He had called me to India, and He would prove faithful in helping me get there. I don't believe He caused me to get into a car accident, but I do believe He used what happened, what was meant to be something bad, for something good (Genesis 50:20).

Some might question how I felt I had the right to go on a mission trip, considering that I'd been disobedient to God (by dating my college beau). What right did I have to tell people about Jesus if I wasn't following him 100 percent? I had no right. I was underqualified and over-ambitious. I was a sinner. I am a sinner. But Jesus broke through my insufficiency. I had Him, and He was and is good enough. No, I didn't study theology and I didn't grow up following God, but I knew my life without Jesus, I knew what Jesus was presently doing in my life, and I was willing to share that. That's all God needs now; that's all God needed from me then. He takes care of the rest just like He took care of the rest then.

College beau and I mutually ended our relationship the day before I left for India. He'd been accepted to graduate school in Utah and would be leaving in August. I was staying in Nebraska, and would only return from India in August, after he'd already moved. We agreed that a long distance relationship would be difficult (though I was willing to try). We maturely said goodbye, but agreed to maintain our friendship, to see each other again soon.

Subtle tears fell from my eyes as I hugged him goodbye. I wanted a good man and he was one, so I thought I would marry this beau one day. Perhaps someday, after graduate school, we would reconnect. I got into my car to drive away, thinking I should be more devastated, because he made me so happy. But there was a different hope that kept me from breaking down. Deep inside I knew that I had a greater strength now, so I could let him go. I was going to be okay.

CHAPTER FOUR

India

I BEAMED.

The humidity from a squelching Texas summer seeped from my pores, found its way upon my cheeks, my forehead. But there was more that caused this glistening on my face. I had just spent approximately five days in Garden Valley, Texas, with my team, training for our trip to India. The departure date had arrived, and we were headed to Houston to board our flight. A school bus, painted in a fading yellow and black, pulled up; a coach bus, with its tinted windows, the sun reflecting off its waxed surface, followed closely behind. My first thought was "there must not be enough room for all of our supplies and luggage on the big bus, so the old school bus is going to haul our remaining things to Houston." This would be the first of many thoughts that would reveal my expectations of privilege.

Our team, consisting of nineteen people, was one of the smallest among the masses of ambition gathered to leave for their various destinations. We, therefore, would be bumping along the interstate—while a larger team would be riding celebrity style to Houston. With no underneath storage capacity in our old school bus, we packed shoulder to sticky shoulder onto the torn leather seats, along with our luggage and supply boxes. Air conditioning wasn't an amenity on this bus. As we opened the windows, I sat

up on the heels of my tennis shoes stretching like a panting ca-
nine for the muggy breeze. I hadn't even left the United States and
already I was feeling uncomfortable.

When we arrived at the airport, I stumbled through the relief-
chilled doors, nearly kissing the waxed floors as the air condi-
tioner greeted me at the Departures wing. Our team of nineteen
was split into smaller groups for accountability and safety. I was
in charge of ensuring that the four girls in my group, along with
myself, my luggage, and two other supply boxes, all got checked
in. We gathered our things and melted into the already-estab-
lished line of passengers waiting to check in. Following the line
in front of me, I inched forward, tapping the heap of boxes and
bags along with my foot, but a little too much force in my scoot
sent my suitcase and the supply boxes crashing down. I hustled
everything back into place, but then I began questioning the logic
of putting me in charge. Maybe my team leader saw something
responsible in me, but as I got the eagle eye from those waiting
around me, the enormity of my responsibility (I was deemed responsible, therefore I could be *held responsible*) gave me the jitters.
"God, I need some of that divine order," I prayed.

I didn't imagine there'd be a Starbucks where we were going so
I grabbed Paris, a dark-haired, Italian-American girl on my team,
and we headed through the airport terminals in search of our last
latte for nearly a month. As we prepared to board the plane for
our nineteen-hour flight to India, I sipped deeply out of my venti
cup for the last precious drops of delight.

Burnt-orange barrenness filled the rounded frame of the airplane
window as our plane descended over the Arabian desert. Then, as
we closed in on the Dubai airport for a layover, it was much like the
switch of a photoshoot backdrop—suddenly, a bustling epicenter

came into view. I disembarked, and found myself swept away by the variety of color and people, each a representative of a distinct cultural group.

Men were dressed in pure white robes and were wearing solid-colored cloth turbans on their heads. If one hears the word *turban* in Nebraska, one thinks one of two things: the towering, white wind turbines that cover the planes of Wyoming, or a turbine engine: men's headwear definitely doesn't come to mind! I was mesmerized. I couldn't help but stare. I'd been to Peru, but it didn't compare to this; I had been younger then and I didn't fully take in my surroundings.

I thought I had been aware of the world's different peoples and cultures (c'mon, I'd watched the world news and the Discovery Channel!), but at that moment I realized I had been naïve, that until then I hadn't fully grasped the level of diversity that actually exists. I suddenly realized that I had spent much of my life seeing the world through tunnel vision, as if the lens of a telescope had been pressed against my eye. Not only had I not seen what surrounded me, due to the walls of the tunnel, but I had only seen what was directly at the mouth of the opening. I'd spent the majority of my life caught up in what was right in front of me, and hadn't explored or experienced anyone or anything truly different from what I already knew. I was humbled by the realization of how small I was and how little I truly knew about the world; I hadn't even begun to breach the surface, to reach the depths of who and what makes up the world in its entirety. This overwhelming realization felt almost as though someone had pressed high voltage prongs against my skin, shooting energy into my nervous system: something that immobilized and electrified me all at the same time.

As we boarded our next plane and began our flight across the Arabian Sea, another wave of revelation washed over me. This place, this very sea, had been just a geographical location on the world globes I'd spun around as I sporadically stopped a finger on all the places I wanted to visit. It was now part of my reality. I was, at that very moment, flying over a place, where only days before my finger had rested on a globe.

We landed in Chennai, India, at roughly 3 a.m. their time, and once again I and our entire team were a minority. It's something to adjust to when your whole life you've been in the majority. Having drunk too much coffee and water, I bolted for the nearest bathroom, which, even though I'd been forewarned, I expected to be just like the restrooms in the U.S.A. Suddenly I screeched to a halt at the open stall door: what was facing me was not what I had expected. With my nose crinkled and my head tilted in bewilderment, I squinted as I pondered, "Now, how do I do this best?" I'd grown-up around farms, so I'd learned how to squat up against a tree or squat in the cornfields, but this just seemed a bit more complicated. Thankfully, in the other stalls there were Western toilets.

In the areas of India where we were going, a "squatty potty," as they're known, is common practice. In the more urban areas, it consists of a hole in a tiled floor with a toilet seat frame around it and footpads on each side of the hole. These traction pads are meant to help prevent one from slipping into the hole (something I would have far too many close calls with on the duration of the trip!). But if you're in rural areas . . . , it's simply a hole in the ground.

The concept is simple: you spread your feet and yes, squat. Each bathroom stall has either a small tap of water on the wall and a small jug or a bucket filled with water for flushing and wiping. The process in Indian culture is to pour a small volume into the cupped left-hand to wash oneself. One's left hand, therefore, is considered unclean, because it serves the purpose of cleaning and wiping oneself in the restroom.

At first, I was nearly brought to tears by the thought of the people in this part of India not having the privileges I did. (Luckily, our mission group had been warned about the lack of toilet paper, so my backpack was stocked like the shelves of an American staple—a Wal-Mart warehouse.)

Later, after my initial shock wore off, I realized that these people didn't want my sympathy—theirs was simply a different culture with a different practice. I began to wonder what made my way the only right way, and if I had any right at all in finding their practices unusual and disgusting. Perhaps my culture's hygiene practices saddened them, because my constant use of toilet paper and large quantities of water could be considered not only wasteful, but environmentally damaging as well. In moments like these, I began to look from God's eyes, rather than just my own. (I found out later that toilet paper is in fact available, it's just not a common practice in the areas we would travel to. But I continued to lug rolls of toilet paper around in my backpack for the duration of the trip!)

Experiencing these contrasting emotions while living temporarily in this foreign place, I was reminded of a book I had read a couple of years prior entitled *The God Chasers,* by Tommy Tenney. In his book, Tenney tells the story of an American pastor who, while speaking to an Ethiopian pastor, states, "Brother, we pray for you in your poverty." The Ethiopian pastor responds to the statement somewhat sadly by saying, "No, you don't understand. We pray for you because it is much harder for you to live at the place God wants you to live in the midst of prosperity, than it is for us in the midst of our poverty."

This statement came back to me, gutted me, shifted, and shook my very reasons for traveling to India. Because of the prosperity I'd lived in all my life, when I began experiencing practices and standards different than my own it was hard for me to live out of a place of humility as opposed to a place of judgment. Mortification and pity were the emotional places I loved from—as opposed to empathy and honor. These particular cultural differences weren't wrong or sinful, and I was certain God required me to view them as they were: just differences. I was also certain He found beauty in the fact that His people, His creation, are so uniquely different: because He intentionally made us that way. I determined that I would look for the beauty in all of India and its uniqueness, regardless of what might make me uncomfortable.

Our team loaded into two fourteen-seater vans to begin the fifteen-hour trek to Nagercoil. We pulled away from the airport. I hadn't seen this level of disparity in living standards ever in my life! The people we passed were in obvious need. The sight of shanties made of corrugated tin, cardboard, and trash afflicted my heart and housed sadness within it. Worse were the torn tarps draped over boxes or boards to create shelter—making the shanties appear luxurious. To use the word "luxurious" to describe a shanty is scandalous, I know, but a shanty was better than those boxes, those torn-up and torn-through tarps.

Cows, considered highly esteemed and holy by many Indians, roamed the roads with an arrogance that reeked like their cow piles. Their back sides bumping up and down as if they knew that no one was going to mince them up and toss them into a casserole. Some roamed and some were chained to trees in front yards, like dogs are found in America. Straw protruded from scarecrows sewn in human form and painted with nightmarish faces. These scarecrows, which were suspended from certain houses like sentries outside Buckingham Palace, were tasked with warning off evil spirits. The sight of them sent a shudder down my spine even after I turned away.

We stopped for about an hour to freshen up and eat breakfast before continuing on to Nagercoil. Our global partners had a contact who selflessly allowed us to rest in her home and who provided us with breakfast. There was no refrigerator, stove, washer, or dryer in this home. Appliances that I considered necessities were not even a part of this household. Food was made on a fire in the backyard and clothes were hung on any railing or place available: just flopped over and left to dry.

I reflected on my refrigerator back home; it was stocked with coffee creamer, Miracle Whip, lunch meat, fruit—all the foods I loved. I fit the description of what our American culture calls a "poor college student," yet even in my lack, I didn't go without. I had considered myself struggling when I couldn't find it within my budget to purchase fabric softener and, here, individuals were living without even the appliance to wash automatically the very clothes I enjoyed softened.

God, again, opened my eyes. I saw myself to be an abundantly privileged person, yet I discovered that I had been abundantly ungrateful. I couldn't help but let my idealistic prayers pour out: "Jesus, wave your hand over this entire region and make things better," I yearned. "Why, God, did you allow me to live how I live?" I questioned. "Why am I not living in this country, suffering like these people are? Why was I born in America, into a life of privilege?" Questions raced through my heart and shook me deeply. I wanted to remove every ounce of materialism I had within me.

The sun was high in the sky when we climbed back into the vans and began heading southwest. Someone told me that the things considered road hazards in a first-world country *are* the road in a third-world country, so I leaned sideways on my seat to look out the windshield at the road we were driving on. It was true: this two-lane paved road, littered with potholes, *was* the hazard. The two lanes often suddenly became three lanes . . . and then randomly shrank down to two again. This wasn't because of the changing infrastructure of the road or the land, though, but simply because of how people were driving: which was however—and wherever!—they decided to. Forget turn-signals or hazard lights; horns honking and arms flailing out windows were signals to other vehicles to get out of the way—now! Also, "car-length cushion" was definitely not a term coined in India.

Once when traffic was at a standstill on that tarmac jungle, I looked out the windshield to see our van pressed clean against the back of the vehicle in front of us-bumper to dented bumper. Mouth gaping, I hyperventilated as our driver attempted to navigate us through a gap as thin as the width of our headlight. Sure there were cars sandwiched around us on all sides, but it was up to them whether to widen the gap or get hit. Forget parting the Red Sea, our driver was about to perform a competing miracle!

I also came to understand drivers in India don't check their mirrors (if they even have them). They only see what's in front of them and then only when it's startlingly in front of them. On the two lane roads, my heart raced as we overtook car after car only to swerve back into our own lane seconds before a collision with oncoming traffic. We weren't driving the speed limit and neither was anyone else. I never saw a speed limit sign and even if I had it would've merely been a road decoration. The speed limit was as fast as a car could go without beginning to shake. When passing cars, it was as fast as the car could go: period! After one too many near-head-on collisions, and constantly thinking that I was only seconds away from dying a martyr's death (and before I even got the chance to tell a single soul about Jesus!)—I decided I would simply keep my eyes glued to the side window beside our seat, enjoy the country-side, and pray like crazy. Maybe I didn't mind living in America so much, after all!

After surviving fifteen hours on the road, our vans finally pulled into Nagercoil a little before 4 a.m. Fourteen of us girls rolled out our sleeping bags on the tiled floor of a room in our host's house and took a three-hour nap before the day officially began. We awoke to a table adorned with bread, jam, scrambled eggs, and fresh bananas. We were also served hot tea with milk (something other than chai) which rolled down my throat and made my belly very happy. Later during our stay, Paris and I requested a cooking lesson on how to make it. I jotted the recipe down in my worn journal. It consisted of merely black tea, milk, sugar, and fresh cardamom, but it would do the trick in curbing our Starbuck's cravings. These tea cups weren't quite the size of my usual venti, so in true Indian tradition I found myself bartering with other teammates for their tea until I'd reached my quota.

Later that first morning, we attended an in-house church service at the home of our host family. This was where they all gathered; this was their church building, and the tiled floors were their pews. Nothing fancy hung on the walls of their home, not even a traditional image of Jesus hanging on a wooden cross. Church consisted of just a few people who gathered on the living room floor, but these few were deeply passionate for Christ. Their native tongue filled the house, their hands and a small drum the only accompaniment. I didn't understand what was being sung, but Jesus was there—the universal Jesus. As they sang, He deposited a deeper love within my heart. I watched them worship with abandon, without any big bands, sound systems, or fancy projectors, and I longed to worship God just like this. Just a voice ringing out, just a hand raised towards heaven, just a heart turned passionately toward Him.

The simple yet profound service ended, and we were told we needed to get traditional clothing before we could begin ministering, especially us women. So after the church service we loaded the vans and headed downtown to shop for our *churidars*. This traditional outfit consists of a wide-cut, one-size-fits-all, cotton pant that narrows at the ankle, and a long, knee-length tunic worn on top.

A lot of the clothing was custom-made, but due to time constraints we went to a shop with options already available. The store owner led us to an area, brought each of us girls a stool to sit on, and began having his workers bring out clothes. I told myself that at least with the purchase of these clothes we would be helping this local shop and the local economy, and I felt slightly less guilty about my past exorbitant clothing purchases. I marveled at the fabrics and colors, finally deciding on a maroon and dark blue churidar, and a hot pink and lime green churidar. I would rotate them every other day.

Nagercoil is cradled between the Western Ghats on all sides. The lush mountain range and fanning palm trees were exactly as I imagined India to be as a little girl. Flooded fields of rice stole my gaze as I watched Indian farm workers, shin-deep in a day's work. The vegetation and rivers were arranged with artistry, as if they'd been hand-placed in their exact location for beauty alone. The landscape painted a spellbinding picture: a wonderment no words of mine could describe, nor would I dare try to trap it on a page.

The city streets painted a very different picture, however.

Public urination in India is both common and frequent. If you see a building, you'll see a man's backside. If you see a tree, you might want to divert your eyes. I was certain that for every landmark I saw, there was the equivalent of a man peeing on the street. Walking down a city street, we witnessed a row of men standing behind a chest-high cement wall. They were looking over the wall out onto the street as if they were just a bunch of anthropologists observing all the hustle. I was tempted to wave . . . until I realized I was staring point-blank at a public urinal: right there! On the street! The stench of urine blended with the medley of spices, and burned my nostrils like a curry. I have a brother, I have step-brothers, and I wondered if the streets of

India might be a little slice of heaven on earth for men. I also wondered if they might be the direct opposite for women.

Because we were walking the streets and not driving them, my eyes were open long enough to get a good look at the city. The shops were stacked one upon the other like a set of building blocks. Vendors, with shared walls of metal and wood, lined the sidewalk, selling fried food, tea, golden images of gods and goddesses, and various other trinkets. Products and services were advertised in Tamil on sun-faded signs painted in vibrant colors of green, pink, and orange. The differences between the countryside and the city were drastic, but surprisingly I didn't find one more beautiful than the other. For all the charm of the landscape, there was something equally enchanting about the buzz of the city.

Our first day of ministry was spent in simply following. We began at a hospital near where we were staying. I knew it would be different than the hospitals I had experienced in the United States, but once again I severely underestimated how different. The floors were cement, and most rooms were accessed from the outside of the building. The patients' beds were worn-out cots that appeared to have been there since the hospital was built—in what year that was, I had no idea. Instead of disposable plastic bags for the patients' IV tubes, glass bottles hung from old fashioned metal stands. The rooms were sectioned off into wards, separating varying levels of sickness. There was no air conditioning or heat, no electronic monitors, no call lights, no private bathroom for each patient. Just rooms filled with tense feelings of sadness, desperation, and hopelessness.

My group of four went to a number of rooms to offer prayer and encouragement. We stepped into a private ward, which was one of the worst I had seen. A middle-aged man suffering from tuberculosis lay on his bed staring at the ceiling. His sister sat by his side. They spoke Tamil, the official language of the state of Tamil

Nadu, but through our translator we discovered that the patient's wife had passed away just two years earlier. He also had two small children still at home. He was very poor, very frightened, and very sick. There was not much we could do but pray. I felt so utterly helpless, but was reminded that the most powerful thing I could do was pray. We underestimate it sometimes; we often think a portion of medicine or money or food is more powerful. However, God has a special burden for the sick and the poor, and the truth was, He would remain present long after our departure.

> "The Lord will sustain him on his sickbed and restore him from his bed of illness."
>
> – Psalm 41:3

The verses God had brought to my heart during Dad's illness were just as powerful, just as relevant, in this situation clear across the world. Though my dad's restoration was completed in Heaven and this man's might be as well, the truth remained that God would sustain him on his sickbed if he cried out to Him.

After a lunch of peanut butter sandwiches (we brought peanut butter from America) and bananas, we continued on to a village where we'd invite people to a service we would put on that evening. It was only the first day and I was already overwhelmed with sight after sight, story after story of sickness, desperation, and heartache. I couldn't imagine how God's heart could bear this weight, this heaviness. I was witnessing such a small amount of the pain of the world, yet I thought that surely my own heart would give way.

The people in this village were a mixture of Christians and Hindus. They were all the most generous and welcoming people I have ever met. As we went door-to-door, floor mats were pulled out and people brought out whatever food they had available. None of us wanted to take their food, partly because of our uncertainty as to what it was, but mostly because they had so very little. However, it was crucial that we accept these offerings, as culturally it was insulting to turn down something offered.

One lady in particular pulled out all the mats she owned, grabbed a banana vine off her floor, which was crawling with ants, and passed it around. After we finished banana number 1, we were strongly encouraged to take banana number 2. So needless to say, we did. We were then served a sort of coffee, which tasted very much like cappuccino, and all of us were ecstatic at this. The Indians have a knack for making excellent coffee and tea! At the next house we visited, we received another cup of hot tea, jackfruit, and cookies.

In my opinion, jackfruit is not the most appetizing fruit. I choked not one, but two pieces down, making the developing fruit bowl in my stomach all the larger. The pastor, who traveled with us, encouraged me to take a handful of the jackfruit and put it in my backpack for later. He also encouraged the rest of the girls to take a handful. Now jackfruit is not a fruit you can take anywhere like an orange or an apple. When it is cut it is wet, unprotected, and sticky—not really something I wanted to chuck into my backpack filled with rationed toilet paper. After some debate, the pastor and the family decided to dump the fruit into a plastic sack and send it with us. I was relieved.

Most of the locals we invited to the service came. We shared the Gospel and prayed individually with people. A few of the girls and I taught the young ones childhood games we were familiar with, such as duck-duck-goose. We listened to their little Indian accents rise above the rest of the crowd as they yelled DUCK! DUCK! GOOSE! I'm certain they loved their new English words and, though I'm not certain they knew what they meant, they knew what to do when they were yelled. It was a comical representation of how we sometimes find ourselves operating in life—running around in circles, bopping people on the head, yelling words we don't fully understand, but whose impact gets a desired result.

At the end of the first day we collapsed into our sleeping bags, fourteen of us girls sleeping side by side. The boys on our team stayed at another host home. At 10 p.m. the lights went out yet, despite our physical exhaustion, sleep evaded us. Paris and I were like little girls at a slumber party. We pulled our pillows close together, told stories, and giggled in our quietest whisper. We talked until our voices gave way to the heaviness of our eyelids; this would become a nightly ritual for our growing friendship. Paris was going to be serving on two mission trips that summer: after our time together in India, she would travel to an orphanage in South Africa to volunteer. I found myself wishing I could go with her.

The following day, we visited another hospital in a neighboring town. More crowded than the previous one, we made lots more visits to all kinds of patients. The ward we were in was lined on both sides of the room with beds. Family members huddled around, clutching their loved ones. There were no separators or partitions between patients, so we moved a few feet at a time from bed to bed. An old man with greasy grey hair, dark eyes, and a faulty walk followed us from person to person, standing off in the background.

We arrived at a bed where a young man lay. The man who'd been following in the background stepped forward, eyes glowing and glossy. This was our grey-haired spectator's grandson, the one whom he wanted prayer for. Having listened and watched us intently with the others, he immediately told the translators that he wanted to know this Man we talked about: he wanted to trust in Jesus. As we prayed for him, tears began to trickle down his wrinkled cheeks and hope began to overcome the shadow of desperation that had not long ago filled his eyes.

And when he finds it, he joyfully puts it on his shoulders and goes home. Then he calls his friends and neighbors together and says, "Rejoice with me; I have found my lost sheep. I tell you that in the same way there will be more rejoicing in heaven over one sinner who repents than over ninety-nine righteous persons who do not need to repent.

– Luke 15:5–7

I was certain there was rejoicing in heaven at that moment over this elderly man's decision. I was certain that Jesus' tears of joy fell along with this man's: merging into the same puddle, sharing in his joy, sharing in his sorrow.

We spent the remainder of the morning at the hospital and then headed to have lunch at a church tucked up in the mountains. There was a nearby village which we would visit later in the afternoon, but for now we were afforded some free time. Paris, Paige, another girl named Holly, and I decided to go for a walk and do some exploring. Paige and the other Holly were a part of our larger service team, though not part of the immediate small group that Paris and I were in. Paige was a petite blonde from the vast state of Texas, with a sense of humor that equaled its size. Holly was the baby of the group, at just 16 years old, and she had become an immediate friend of mine and Paris. We called ourselves "Double-P.H.", short for Paris, Paige, and two Hollys. Maybe we were acting a little immature, but when girls of any age all get together something young, something vibrant, spills out.

On our exploration, we stumbled across what appeared to be a school building and a group of children playing outside. Upon seeing us, a slender Indian man who was monitoring the children invited us to come meet them: and not just these children, but the entire school! One of our translators, who had been following from a distance, ran to catch up when he saw this new opportunity. We were shown to the school manager's office to enjoy some tea while the teachers gathered all the students into one room. Somewhere between fifty and sixty children would be our next audience to witness to. Since we didn't really have anything prepared, the four of us (Double-P.H.) decided to teach them a few songs: "Deep and Wide," "He's Got the Whole World in His Hands," and "Father Abraham." After that we would interact with them to explain, on a deeper level, what the songs were all about.

It was a God-appointment for sure, that this was even allowed in this particular school, however it wasn't easily understood. Hindus have 330 million deities, but believe they are all a manifestation of the one absolute God, Brahman, and don't advocate worshiping just one God. Despite what they'd been raised in, we were sent to share the Truth in love, that this God of ours was the One and the only God you need. No, we couldn't argue until our faces turned blue, we couldn't judge them or point fingers; but we did what we could: we told the Truth, loved them in Truth, and trusted God to water the seeds we planted on that schoolyard that day.

On our way back to meet the rest of our team, we joked we were the "true" missionaries—that while the rest relaxed, we were busy "fighting the good fight." It was by no means true, but we kidded about our righteousness. Looking back, I see we were just that, still somewhat like kids in our faith and perspective.

In the evenings, we often had dinner at our host house and other times we were invited to various other homes; welcomed as if we were the most special of guests. In one particular home, after dinner, the Indian women put henna blossoms, fragrant white flowers, in our hair. They drew with henna on our hands, lightly staining them with orangish-red flower designs.

The scent of the henna blossoms was so strong, so overpowering, it seemed as though my entire body was perfumed—simply because they were in my hair. In that moment, I didn't realize the significance. Just as we were being adorned in beauty, I was obtaining a context for how Christ's beauty is depicted. And there was that depiction, in Song of Solomon when the lover describes her beloved as a cluster of henna blossoms, "My beloved to me is a cluster of henna blossoms from the vineyards of En Gedi" (Song of Solomon 1:14).

En Gedi is one of two fresh-water springs on the western shore of the Dead Sea. An oasis, a sanctuary, likened to a paradise. In Bible times it was well known for its lush vineyards, for being an agricultural center. When the lover described her beloved, she likened him to henna blossoms; a perfumed fragrance, which represented beauty. He smelled lovely to her, but not just lovely: fragrant in the sense that he smelled like a cluster of henna blossoms that came, not from just any garden, but from paradise. He excited her pleasures, her senses, her deepest desires. The first chapter in Song of Solomon depicts the longing for intimacy with the beloved. The lover pours her heart out completely to him.

In India, henna blossoms in my hair, their fragrance engulfing me, I was beginning to desire a deeper intimacy with my God, as I began to see His beauty: how He enticed my deepest desires and caused my senses to explode. I understood the beauty and fragrance of a henna blossom, and I was beginning to understand the beauty of the fragrance of intimacy with Christ.

By the fourth day of ministry, I hated squatty potties. Every time I used one, I found myself off-balance and nearly slipping into the hole. I would spend the time before entering the battle arena self-motivating, only to emerge with wet pant legs and burning thigh muscles. Because the cotton-pants were one-size fits all, they were like a parachute. I stretched them as far in front of me as I could in an attempt to keep them dry, but it never worked.

During this process on one particular day, I heard a startling and prolonged *riiiiiiip*; as if someone played a musical formata over a note. You all know that "oh, no" ripping sound. I pulled my parachute pants up, only to find that I'd ripped the seam straight down the crotch. And my day had hardly begun! Not only that, but I'd also soaked my tunic. Thankfully, this knee-length top, though it was wet, covered the hole in my pants. I cursed in my head (I wasn't going to allow my team members to hear that through the thin, wood door). I cursed the hole in those pants and I cursed that squatty potty. I could've kicked that bucket of water over, I was so mad.

Each day we traveled to different villages and were welcomed into petite cement dwellings beneath golden rooftops of thatch. Some ventures were nearby and easily accessible, while others required an hour's drive or longer. For those villages that were tucked into the mountains, we drove as far as possible and then hiked the remainder of the way through the rugged jungle. We hiked to His Indian children just as Jesus hiked to save us. Once there, we encouraged, we loved, we told them about the Jesus whose hope was active, was alive, was resurrected. Our translators and global partners, who were nationals themselves, would connect with those who wanted to know more about Christ or who needed help. They would take over helping these individuals and reconnecting with them once we left. This follow-up was crucial.

To travel through India, meeting people, witnessing to them, and then leaving them without connections or resources would have been of no benefit at all. Having locals who were able to help get them the support they needed was important. We could assist, but these nationals were the ones who would finish the work.

On one ministry day, we traveled the steep and winding roads to an orphanage that housed over 200 children between the ages of four and seventeen. The main building was nestled on top of a mountain. Dome-shaped and made of wood, windows that lined the full circumference of the building allowed one to look out at the facilities below. Other buildings were staggered around the area—some sleeping quarters, some classrooms. Due to the sheer number of children, the orphanage could have been a village itself. One member of our team mentioned how amazing it was that God took children who were unwanted or couldn't be cared for, and, just like a mother tucking them safely into bed, He tucked them away among the mountains, amidst the beauty of His creation. I saw Father God again and again as a protective Daddy not out to harm us, but out to heal us, love us, and care for us.

The children loved holding hands, and they ran to grasp any hand of ours within reach. One little boy, who was about four years old, had a death grip on mine; so much so, that he ended up following me everywhere I went because he simply would not let go. It broke my heart; my heart ached for him and the other orphans, ached in the sense of actually, physically, feeling pain in my heart. This little boy and all of these children needed so much more than a hand to hold. They needed a mommy and a daddy: ones who would affirm them, cling to them just as tightly, and reassure them of their love. Just the thought that each of these children lay in bed at night dreaming of what it might be like to experience a mother's hug or the proud smile of a father was enough to make me want to adopt as many as humanly possible. But that still wouldn't have been enough, because I knew that the number of orphans just on the Indian sub-continent alone was staggering, and the number of orphans worldwide is a catastrophe.

In 2011, UNICEF estimated that the number of orphaned children below age seventeen worldwide (both of whose parents have died due to any cause) was approximately 17.9 million. UNICEF also defines orphans as children who have lost one parent or both parents, and that total number reaches an estimate of 151 million. 151 million children in the world have lost one or both parents:

they have lost a parent, just like me, just like many of you. It's a tremendous, an unfathomable amount of loss, of grief. There are organizations out there trying to provide help, to provide hope. But are we? Are we joining their forces?

Aside from that, let's pause for a moment over the fact that 17.9 million young hearts are crying out because they've lost both parents. Because they need parents. The echoes of 17.9 million voices are asking, "Does anybody love me? Why doesn't anyone want me?" I can only imagine if God answered us the way I—the way we collectively—often answer their cries, whether we say it out loud or in our inner dialogue:

"I just want my own."

"I don't want to take on someone else's."

"They may have severe behavioral issues; it's irresponsible."

"I'm not ready."

In the beginning, God picked His people. They were the Jews, the chosen ones—His own. But God knew our voices would be crying out. His heart broke for us before Jesus even walked the earth, and He knew He could no longer just call the Jews His children. He had to pour out His love on us, the Gentiles too. We had severe behavioral issues then, we have severe behavioral issues now. I look back at myself after I became a Christian, and I behaved shockingly at times; I look at myself now, and I behave shockingly at times. Every protective command that flows from the mouth of God, I've first tried to reason my way around. Yet, He saw my need, He sees our need. Should we not have that same heart for other lost children?

> For He chose us in Him before the creation of the world
> to be holy and blameless in his sight. In love He predes-
> tined us to be adopted as His sons through Jesus Christ,
> in accordance with his pleasure and will-to the praise of

His glorious grace, which He has freely given us in the
One he loves.

– Ephesians 1:4–6

God loved these children, His heart longed for them. So I loved
these children, not because I was holy, but because He placed His
heart for them inside of me. His heart quickened for them, so my
heart quickened for them.

Shortly after we left the orphanage, we stopped at one of
Compassion International's sites to help serve the children food.
Compassion International is a child sponsorship program that provides meals and education to children around the world. Having
heard of it in the States, it was wonderful to see, first-hand, the
work being done in another country. Sponsored children were
truly being blessed by their sponsor's monthly donations.

Day after day my heart was breaking: breaking for the children, breaking for the people. I asked the same questions so many
have asked, "God, why are there so many orphans? Why are there
so many hurting?" "Why are there so many poor?" "You're an all-
powerful God, why?" I'm reminded of a quote I read in Francis
Chan's book *Crazy Love* in which an individual asks God those
same questions, "Why, God?" God tenderly looks at the man and
in a gentle rebuke says, "You ask me why. But, I, also, ask you why?"
God can so easily do something about the problem. However, we,
the people who occupy this earth, can as well. If we are God's
temples, if the All-Powerful lives inside us, we are also—in His
strength—all-powerful to evoke change.

After this particular orphanage, we journeyed to the village of Kottilpadu, which had been badly hit by the 2004 Indian
Ocean tsunami. Four years after the event, the people were still
scarred by grief. The stories of the lost ricocheted off the ocean
and echoed from nearly every household. In one home, a man

was caring for his only daughter. He'd lost his wife. In another home, a little boy told the story of losing his two younger sisters who could not swim. He watched those hellish waves sweep them away. In home after home, people vividly recalled that day; they remembered those they had lost. I mentally envisioned all the tears cried over those last four years and the tears that would continue to fall in their loved ones' memory, all accumulating to once again flood that community. My own loss seemed so small compared to theirs, but it was just as real.

For a couple of days we diverted from our usual daily ministry to one of a more physical nature, the building of a home for the elderly in Mangalakuntu, a town roughly a forty-minute drive from Nagercoil. In Indian culture, children typically take their aging parents into their own home and care for them until their death. However, on occasion, aged individuals are left with no one to care for them, and thus, nowhere to go. This particular facility was being built by a church to fill that need. Being near completion, but still needing a lot of work, it already housed ten to fifteen individuals.

We spent our time hauling dirt, helping the hired workers, planting coconut trees, and visiting the elderly. One job in particular was to help the hired workers—who had been hired from a nearby village—build a brick wall. As a group of us were helping the stone masons and the work was quickly getting done, it crossed my mind that maybe our help wasn't as beneficial as seemed at first sight. After all, as soon as the work was finished, they would be out of a job. And these were people desperate for money, so less time working meant they would ultimately get paid less.

I was disturbed by this thought, so I grabbed one of the pastors and asked him about it. He said that, yes, the workers would ultimately get paid less because of our help, but the church was the one paying them, so we were saving the church money in the end. Not sure how I felt about that answer, I continued with my questions. "How much do the workers earn per day?"

"The masons make 350 rupees, the rest, 250," he replied.

I did some quick calculations in my head; the masons made nearly $8.75 U.S. dollars per day and the other workers roughly $6.75 per day. The $6.75 full day's wage for hard, physical labor amounts to less than what an American adult would make per hour at a minimum wage job in the United States.

The pastor went on to explain that the average village worker typically only earned somewhere between 60 and 100 rupees for a day's work, or $1.50 to $2.50. Bug-eyed, I shook my head in disbelief. Torn between wanting to slack off so the laborers could be employed longer, yet also wanting to help the church finish this important project, I continued lugging bricks, but slower than before. My hope was that the following day I would be too sore to work even that fast, and then I could have a genuine reason for my slower pace.

With only three days left of our ministry, we traveled to another village surrounded by fields and fields of wind turbines. The wind beat against my churidar with such ferocity that I thought my parachute pants were going to lift off! When we arrived at the local church, they presented us with coconuts. As I mentioned before, I dislike coconut. Though I can stand the meat inside, I *really* dislike coconut milk. But, to get to the meat, one has to drink the milk so the coconut can be whacked open with a machete. I'd already been handed countless coconuts since I'd arrived in India, and by now my belly was swimming and my face was green. One local gentleman was already whacking open everyone else's coconuts. He kept coming to mine, taking it from my hands, shaking it, and handing it back to me as if to say, "Drink up!" I was trying to drink up; I gagged multiple times, but finally finished the entire coconut.

In the yard of the church, one lady sat with chains shackled around her ankles. Born mentally challenged, she sat idly and stared off into the distance. There was no medicine here to help, no facility to care for her, it seemed her life ventures may have been as limited as the chain's length she was restrained by. It absolutely broke my heart. But here, they didn't know any other way; this was the village doing the best they knew how.

Our next stop was to a Stepping Stones Center, which was overseen by one of our global partner pastors, and is a ministry of Serve India Ministries. The Stepping Stone Centers seek to break the cycle of child labor. It's a generational cycle that is uneasily broken, as families are unable to escape the grips of poverty. Children are often forced to quit school and work, or are married off to potential suitors. Through free after-school tutoring, the center seeks to help children with their education and to encourage them to continue with schooling. If a child is struggling and doing poorly in school, they run the risk of being pulled out and forced to work to help contribute to the family's income. The Stepping Stone Centers seek to mentor the children as well as teach them life skills and biblical values.

Though our time with this organization was short, I was blown away by the impact just a few people can have when joining forces. The Stepping Stone Centers are unlocking the shackles of a generation, one cuff at a time, through education and through introducing them to Jesus, who sets the captive free.

Our time in India was at an end and, as much as I didn't want to leave, I was ready to get back to the States and start making a difference. While we were driving to a ministry destination days earlier, a name and an idea had suddenly entered my mind: an idea for an organization whose main focus would be to impact the overlooked, as well as the name of that organization. I knew it could take years, if not a decade, before I looked into starting that organization, but I could start helping people immediately, making a difference with one small act at a time.

After a full day of driving through the Indian countryside on the journey back home, we arrived at an old boarding school where we would spend the night. I could almost hear the pitter-patter of students' feet on the now deserted staircase. This time when we reached our room, instead of finding a place to sleep on a cement floor, we were delighted to find row after row of metal-framed beds. No mattresses, just a metal platform welded to the headboard and footboard and with dark green paint peeling off, but we made them our own as we unrolled our sleeping bags for the night.

The room was surrounded on all sides by a wraparound balcony that overlooked what might have once been an exotic garden. Drained and crumbling, an old fountain stood in the middle, like a tombstone amidst parched grass. I was certain it was a memorial to a once remarkable sight. Later that night we held a worship service on that wraparound balcony. Nineteen of us, along with our leaders, sang out to the lone accompaniment of a guitar. I stood at the edge of the balcony peering up at the trillions of stars shining down on the garden that no longer existed.

It was that night, on that wraparound balcony, when I decided I wanted to be the woman that God wanted me to be. Having previously been so caught up in men and in the pursuit of falling in love, I made a commitment to God not to date *anyone* until after I finished graduate school. I vowed to wait and focus on finishing my education, while trusting my Heavenly Father for a godly, sold-out-for-Christ man. I vowed that I would spend my entire next school year devotedly pursuing Jesus, discovering who I fully was in Him and falling in love with Him, and Him alone. I determined that I was going to let Him write my love story—just like I'd read in the book.

CHAPTER FIVE

Falling Ten Times and Getting Up Ten Times

I WAS ON FIRE.

I burned for God like the flames that would leap up and lick the sides of our cast iron wood-burning stove during the Nebraska winter months when I was younger. To be living in a third world country, helping the impoverished—that was what I wanted. It was all I wanted. I wanted to be uncomfortable for God. Can you believe that? I was tired of living a comfortable life, and was ready to forego my expensive coffees and my pampering sessions.

My hair was getting darker, and the bleach-blonde highlights were becoming more frequent and more expensive to maintain. Plus, for the cost of just one highlight I could help a lot of people, so I dyed my hair dark brown, brushed my hands together, and solved that problem: changing the world, one less highlight at a time!

I wanted to witness God do big things, to change a life with a prayer and through my open hands. I didn't want to go back to my normal life; I wanted that radical life, that all-for-Jesus-or-nothing-at-all life. For some reason, I didn't yet understand that I could live that all-for-Jesus-or-nothing-at-all life right where I was: that God could do big things in my current circumstances.

As the heat of the summer months once again eased into the cooldown of late August, the new school year began. Now I couldn't lose myself in the dirt-caked hands of the orphan or the heaving work of lugging bricks; I had registered to do my master's degree in business administration and accounting, and there were case studies, projects, and exams demanding that I lose myself in them.

Graduate school was challenging. I would put on a fresh pot of coffee at 11 p.m., and not just a half-pot—a full ten-cupper. I had test anxiety, project anxiety, homework anxiety, future career anxiety; I was a muddled up mess of anxiety. 1 Peter 5:7 became my new favorite verse: "Cast all your anxiety on Him, because He cares for you." I was more than willing to chuck that anxiety right up to Heaven and into God's burly arms. My challenge was chucking it up there and trusting that He had me: trusting that He was in control.

I loved learning, I loved being challenged, but I had to pray myself through it. "Jesus, I glorify you," I'd proclaim as I'd lay hands on my textbook like I was going to raise those dead words right off the page and into my spinning brain. As I highlighted my books and went back over my notes, I prayed for supernatural recollection. I had committed to something and I would finish it, though my heart remained forever buried in the wide-eyed faces of the less fortunate, not within the 10-point font of my accounting books.

I spent my time studying in the over-cushioned booths at Barista's Daily Grind, right off West 24th street and across from campus. I would sit cross-legged in the booths at Panera Bread, inhaling the constant aroma of ground coffee beans and way too many carbs. And yes, I was trying to choose less frivolous coffees. I sat on the cold, hard-backed chairs at the university library, which didn't lock its doors until midnight, sipping vending machine coffee and working through assignments. (See: I was sipping *vending machine coffee!*) As my fingertips began frequenting my eyelids and I found myself continually counting the pages left to read or the pages left to type, I would permit myself to dream: dream about what else God might do, what He might use this degree for. I was determined that He would *delicately braid together my love for the less fortunate with business.* Somehow.

Two months into graduate school, I had broken the vow I'd so ambitiously made on that wraparound balcony on that starlit night in India. I'd broken the vow of pursuing only Jesus and waiting for my Jesus-man, my godly man. I thought if I wasn't pursuing men I could live happily, uninterrupted in my singleness and devotion to God. It had never occurred to me that I hadn't developed a strategy to steer clear of men if they pursued me. My whole graduate program revolved around strategy, so why hadn't I thought to develop this one?

I had been doing so well, but men were coming out of the woodworks! This had never really happened to me before. I truly was trying to immerse myself in God's word and to seek Him when I felt lonely, but the enemy kept slyly whispering, *"God isn't the same as a lover. His company isn't enough. You're buying into an idea that's all fluff, and not practical. How can God really meet your needs? And maybe one of **these** men is your Jesus-man. Maybe you're meant to save him, to bring him to Christ."* So what was originally an innocent idea of just friendship, talking, and inviting to church became absolute spiritual destruction.

After only four months of being back in the States, I was at my absolute worst. "Again, Holly?" you ask. Yes, again. I became a totally different person; I outright and forcefully went against what I knew to be God's best for me. I lied to those around me, those Christian friends around me, because how could I let them know that this so-called "changed" girl had fallen so low—could fall so low—after what she'd experienced. The warm embrace of sin welcomed me, and it provided an escape from the stresses and pressures of class. Compromise by tiny compromise, I changed. The change that occurred gutted me emotionally. I knew that what I was doing was wrong, and I became depressed again. I would crawl deep underneath my microfiber comforter, with my arms and legs sprawled out in desperation, as black rivers of tears ran down my cheeks until I tasted their saltiness. I would remember how God had called me to be salt and light in the world. "You are the salt of the earth, but if the salt loses its saltiness, how can it be made salty again? . . . You are the light of the world. A town built on a hill cannot be hidden" (Matthew 5:13–14).

I was losing that saltiness and I was losing the light. I felt it. I knew it.

At the onset of my rebellion, I had begun applying for jobs at audit firms throughout the Midwest. I posted my resume on our university's career services website, and soon received a letter in the mail inviting me to interview on campus with an audit firm located in Cheyenne, Wyoming. A representative would come to my university campus for the first round of interviews and, if I made the second round, I would then be invited out to Cheyenne for more.

The day before my interview was scheduled, I stopped into one of the local Vietnamese nail salons. This was something I'd previously determined that I would never do again, because I was living frugally. The tropical décor inside was meant to depict an island paradise: a getaway in uptown Kearney, Nebraska. Fake palm trees stood above row after row of massage chairs and foot baths. Neon flowers and leis were strewn across cabinets filled with every imaginable color of nail polish. I found a seat, nudging into the center of the assembly line of women with fanned-out fingers. Even though this wasn't a real tropical paradise, for us women it was a getaway. One small touch to my hand felt like a full-on massage, as if it could melt all my stress away. As the technician painted white-tips onto what she could salvage of my chewed-up nails, I wondered if this would be enough; if I would be enough.

I could put on my black suit and walk in with my pristine appearance and subtly spritzed smell (I'd learned all the interviewing tricks at school), but would it be enough? I could google information and rehearse practice interview questions, but at the end of the day, would they want me? Wasn't that one of the questions I'd been asking all along? The question I'd asked over and over again—and not just in reference to a career, but in reference to a man, in reference to Jesus. Does he, do they, could he, would they—want me? At the end of the day, am I enough? Am I pretty enough, am I thin enough, am I smart enough, am I holy enough, am I deep enough, am I funny enough, am I kind enough? I could get lost in a life of efficiency, status, and accomplishment in order to be enough.

There's a medical term for the fear of imperfection or the fear of not being good enough. It's called *atelophobia*, and it's classified as an anxiety disorder. This fear can plague people to the point of a phobia, but this fear doesn't just plague people somewhere out there who we don't know. It plagues me, it may plague you too—just to varying degrees. Do you know what the sad thing is about most individuals who develop atelophobia and other phobias? They are often highly intelligent and possess many talents and capabilities, but they don't see their own talent and intellect because their definition of "good enough" is distorted. So what does "enough" mean, anyhow? And who defines it? And does it really mean ticking all the boxes; being everything? *Enough*, according to the dictionary, means "adequate for the want or need" or "sufficient for the purpose."

"Oh, I'm full. I've had enough food!" (Sure, there's plenty more delicious food, but that was adequate for my wants now, for my needs now.)

> Moses said to the Lord, "Pardon your servant, Lord. I have
> never been eloquent, neither in the past nor since you have
> spoken to your servant. I am slow of speech and tongue.

The Lord said to him, "Who gave human beings their mouth? Who makes them deaf or mute? Who gives them sight or makes them blind? Is it not I, the Lord? Now go; I will help you speak and will teach you what to say."

– Exodus 4:13–14

Sufficient for the purpose. Enough.

I didn't have atelophobia and I imagine you don't either, but out of my fear of not being enough, I was *striving* to be enough. I resorted to doing whatever it took to be enough. Some individuals resort to doing nothing at all, resigning themselves to stop all efforts because after all (they think), they won't measure up.

I knew the story of Martha and Mary in the Bible, and I knew the message behind it. Martha rushed around in a state of frenzy, trying to prepare the house and the meal for Jesus. Mary sat at Jesus' feet, listening to what He said. Martha got upset because she thought Mary was lazy. Jesus rebuked Martha: "You are worried and upset about many things, but few things are needed—or indeed only one. Mary has chosen what is better, and it will not be taken away from her" (Luke 10:41–42).

I knew the story, but I struggled with it. I told myself that I would sit at Jesus' feet and listen. I made it a point not to strive; in fact I focused so hard on not striving that I discovered that in itself, *that* was striving—I was striving not to strive! How could I know this scripture, know this lesson, and still not be able to apply it? Because I knew the scripture, but I didn't *know* that One Thing: Jesus. I knew a *remnant* of who Jesus is. My revelation of who Jesus is was only a small fraction of who He truly is. Like Martha, I spent so much time serving Jesus that I didn't sit down and listen to Him, to really get to know Him through scripture. Would I just allow myself to say, "Forget it all—I love you, Jesus!

Forget it all—you're enough Jesus; and because you're enough, I'm enough! I am enough!"

> But he said to me, "My grace is sufficient for you, for my power is made perfect in weakness." Therefore, I will boast all the more gladly about my weaknesses, so that Christ's power may rest on me.
>
> – 2 Corinthians 12:9

I'm sufficient; we're sufficient for the purpose; we're adequate for the need, because Christ is.

The time for the interview finally arrived. I walked down a few small steps and into a drab room on campus. A middle-aged woman with dark brown hair and a tailored suit shook my hand and we sat down to begin. *Just be yourself,* I thought. *You know the politically correct answers, but just be yourself.*

The next day I received a phone call inviting me to the second round of interviews in Cheyenne on the following Thursday. The next Thursday morning, I stopped back by the nail salon for another manicure on my way out of town. I didn't have to be in Cheyenne until that evening, for a social and dinner. Since the drive was five hours long, I grabbed a coffee and hit the road with my thoughts about the future packed and ready to be unpacked as the miles passed.

It was October and fall had settled in, drying up the harvest's left-over corn stalks. I drove west, into Mountain Standard Time, golden seas of corn filling my view. As I set my car clock backwards an hour, I contemplated all the backward steps I'd taken in my life. By the time I reached Wyoming and checked into my hotel, I was ready for a new beginning.

The social that evening went well, as did the following day at the firm. I was all nerves, but prayed under my breath the entire time. I didn't know if I wanted the job or didn't want the job. I just wanted *a* job and somewhere to go after graduation. Most important though, I really wanted the job God had for me, that God could use to grow me and challenge me. As Friday's session came to an end, I asked around for the nearest coffee shop. I figured I would, of course, need a strong coffee for the drive home, especially since it would be dark before I made it back. It turned out there was a small, corner coffee shop and book store across the street from the firm, so I headed in that direction.

I crossed the street to the City News and Pipe Shop on the corner of West 18th street and Carey Avenue. One couldn't miss it: its wintergreen window awnings and vintage lighted sign were clearly marked "City News." It was a tobacco shop, book shop, coffee shop, and deli all in one. I ordered a vanilla latte and as I waited, I peered through the window to the street outside. Cheyenne was bigger than my hometown and college town, and definitely had an air of western culture. It was home to Cheyenne Frontier Days; the "Daddy of 'em All" Rodeo, the world's largest outdoor rodeo and Western celebration. I wasn't sure I was the rodeo-girl type, and as much as Cheyenne wasn't where I expected to end up, as I peered out the window of that coffee shop and down the street, I thought I could make it there—if that's what God wanted.

A week after my second interview, I received an offer of employment from the auditing firm in Cheyenne. I hadn't even technically applied to work at the firm, but I had peace about accepting the offer. Despite the lack of peace in my relationships and in the circumstances I'd placed myself in, I had peace there. I would be moving to Cheyenne, Wyoming, in July 2009 to begin my career as an auditor.

After I accepted the offer, I began thinking about the orphanage in South Africa that Paris had told me about when we were in India. My heartbeat quickened every time I thought about volunteering in the orphanage. I began dreaming about Africa, dreaming about orphans. Unable to ignore the urge any longer, I visited the orphanage's website, emailed them for an application, and submitted it. I would graduate in May but would not begin working in Wyoming until July, so I figured I could spend six weeks in South Africa.

My rebellion ended not long after my acceptance to volunteer at the orphanage in South Africa. But I still felt I wasn't worthy enough for the opportunity. *Would I ever get things right? Would I ever be able to live by the Bible? Would I ever be whom God wanted me to be?* I had been so passionate, so ambitious, but just as a candlestick is blown out with one deep and quick breath, my passion and ambition for God had been stifled. *Would I ever be able to take consecutive steps forward without taking steps backwards?* I wondered all these things.

While I questioned myself, I cried out to God. From the depths of my soul, I cried out to the depths of His, because I knew my own vows, my own striving and attempts at trying to be good enough, to do enough, were filthy rags without Him. Not until He absolutely ravished my soul did I grasp that there was absolutely nothing I could do to make myself enough. There was nothing I could do, say, or vow that would make me pure or righteous. I was already all wonderful things to Him. I was already beautiful to Him, lovely to Him; and that had to seep into my soul until I was soaked by it, until I was marked by His love.

In the book of Hosea, God tells the prophet to marry a prostitute named Gomer. Hosea marries her and they have children. Gomer also has children by other men, and three times she leaves Hosea to go back into prostitution, enticed by the luxuries lavished on her by other men. Three times God tells Hosea to go and get her, to bring her back to him. Three times Hosea brings her back.

This story is a depiction of God's love for rebellious Israel and a depiction of God's love for us: His relentless love for us rebellious people, us blatant and intentional sinners. It's a picture of His relentless love for *this* blatant and intentional sinner. And so He took me back. Again.

From January until the end of the school year in May, I kept the remainder of my vow to God—I didn't date. This time it wasn't a checkbox to tick. It wasn't what I needed to do to be good enough or holy enough or Christian enough. It was God's grace and it was what I needed. I had a death-grip on God, because I felt that if I loosened up, I'd lose it all. It was His grace that kept me holding on. I wasn't seeking God in some big experience or big trip like I'd done in the past, like I'd done when I first applied to go to South Africa. I was clinging to Him, seeking Him everywhere, through everything.

I graduated from college in May. I was finally, officially done. It seemed surreal. When I looked back upon my first few days at college, when I was a wide-eyed eighteen-year-old, I remembered crying every single day. I would sit at my desk, in my unfamiliar dorm room, questioning whether I would really make it, or if I would just drop out at semester-end and go back home. I had endured five years and waded through many summer classes. As I crossed the stage that day, I couldn't believe that this phase of my life was over, but I was ready for it to be over. So ready, in fact, that I moved my stuff out of my apartment and into Mom and my step-dad, Jim's, house in Doniphan, Nebraska the following day, and then boarded the plane to South Africa exactly four days thereafter—having no idea what God had in store.

CHAPTER SIX

South Africa

I HUNGERED.

Like the rumbling of an empty stomach, my inner being growled for Africa. A physical yearning for a continent whose land I'd not yet set foot upon crept through me.

When as a little girl I picked at my plate of food, proclaiming that I wasn't going to eat what was in front of me, Mom demanded I sit at the dinner table until it was finished. I'd have to sit there until I finished my dinner because there were starving children in Africa, and I was one lucky girl to have a plate full of food in front of me. I stared deep into the untouched meal on my plate and wondered why, if there were starving children in Africa, we just didn't send all the leftovers, from all the dinner tables in the world, to them. I was certain there were other little girls and boys who would be more than happy to scrape their plates into a box and mail it straight over. One evening I discovered that wasn't a very good idea, however, because the food would be spoiled by the time it arrived. Why then, did Mom keep telling me to finish my plate because they were starving? If they were starving, what did clearing my plate have to do with any of it? It just meant I got to enjoy something they couldn't. I appreciated my food, but what did appreciating it have to do with finishing it? I announced that I wasn't going to clear my plate—period! So I spent a number of evenings alone at the dinner table, foregoing the land of adventure that awaited me outdoors. I knew that Mom wouldn't extend my bedtime, even in the midst of our battle, so I would patiently wait until she caved and sent me to go put on my pajamas.

And I never really stopped wanting to feed those African children. The Africa my plane touched down upon, however, was an Africa that didn't fit into the box I had constructed to define it. We landed on a paved tarmac that fed into a gleaming airport far different from the unpaved, dirt runway and shanty building I'd imagined. In fact, from the moment I put my foot down on the red South African soil, nothing was as I had imagined.

After going through customs, I stepped out into the circular waiting area where a colorful mass of individuals stood holding signs with scribbled names. I circled to and fro, looking for the individuals who ran the orphanage. They were supposed to pick me up. The crowd dwindled from the masses to a scattered few, and after forty-five minutes I began to get a bit worried. *Had they forgotten about me?*

Not knowing what else to do, I pulled my laptop out of my backpack and bought an hour's worth of wi-fi. Then I sat there, huddled on a bench, searching through my email correspondence from the couple. Finally, I came to an email that included a cell-phone number and I quickly jotted it down.

I asked a dark-skinned, middle-aged airport worker where the nearest payphone was and how to use it. I hadn't exchanged any dollars for rand yet, so he dug into his pockets for the necessary coins. This was not quite how I had envisioned my first encounter with "starving" Africans—borrowing money from them!

After a few rings, the director of the orphanage picked up. She hadn't forgotten about me, but her car had gotten a flat tire on the way to the airport, so she was currently stranded. Knowing of no way to contact me, she had simply said a prayer. She and her husband would be at the airport as soon as possible.

We drove on a smooth-surfaced, three-lane highway. Steel-and-glass buildings rose in the distance. Cars, not carts pulled by donkeys as in India, whizzed past us. When we headed onto neighborhood streets, I noticed the houses. Every single house was surrounded by eight-foot-high walls: some made of cement and others made of metal bars fastened together. Barbed wire lined the top of some walls, shards of glass others. Sharp-tipped iron protruded from the tops of yet others. Signs were plastered on nearly every wall, indicating which security system guarded the house: Chubb, ADT, TSS Tactical. Guard shacks stood in many neighborhoods; when the security guards weren't sitting in them, they were patrolling up and down the street, often on bicycles.

When did these walls go up? I wondered. *When did this become a city of fortified houses?* The walls had always been up, I learned, but they got higher as the crime rate did. I knew that crime often increases as unemployment does, and I didn't need anyone to tell me that unemployment was high here. Beggars in tattered clothes stood with open hands and pleading eyes at nearly every traffic light. Women with babies strapped to their backs by a blanket or towel walked from car window to car window; "Please, I have children," they begged.

On average, around 50 people are murdered each day in South Africa. The world average rate for murder is 6.9 per 100,000 people; in South Africa it's 30 per 100,000. Some 66,000 rapes and other sexual assaults are reported each year—those are just the ones reported. Roughly 10,000 hijackings occur each year and roughly 60,000 motor vehicles and bicycles are stolen. Street and public robberies are also approximately 60,000 per year. Nearly 18,000 incidences of home robberies—people being attacked by armed gangs while in their homes—are reported on a yearly basis. On average, 49 households in South Africa are attacked each day.

I stared out the windows as we drove. My heart quickened. I felt alive. I had learned some of these crime statistics before I left the United States, and though they scared me, they didn't deter me. This was where I wanted to be. In the heart of it all, my heart felt it all.

Upon arriving at the orphanage, I settled into the guest flat a few steps away. The combination living room and kitchen contained wicker furniture with bright, floral-print cushions, a small fridge, an electric kettle, and a toaster. The bedroom was furnished with two single beds, covered in zebra-print comforters. African-themed decorations hung on the walls and an armoire stood near the doorway. This, hands down, beat the tiled floor and mat I'd slept on in India. And toilet paper and Western toilets were in abundance!

This trip would clearly be much different than India. And here I'd spend all of my time in the same orphanage.

When I arrived at the home awhile later, I was introduced to the children and their stories.[1] Lebo, a three-year-old girl with big dark eyes, stood feistily before me. She had been abandoned at her *crèche* (the South African term for a day care center). One day her mom had dropped her off and just never returned. The lady who ran the crèche took her home with her for a few days, but after no signs of the mother's return, she had called social services. Social workers picked Lebo up and brought her to the orphanage, where she'd remained the last few months. Her mother had come back into the picture with hopes of getting her daughter back, and had gotten in touch with the social worker assigned to the case. Lebo

---

1   In order to protect the children, I have changed all of their names to different African names.

had not been orphaned after all, just temporarily abandoned. I prayed it would be the last time.

Sechaba, a five-month-old little boy, had been abandoned at the hospital after birth and brought to the Haven—not much of his story was known. He smiled a smile that caught that tender spot in my heart. I could tickle his chin, rub up against his cheek, and be pulled straight into love by his cooing. How a mother could walk right out of the hospital doors and leave him behind in his cot boggled my mind—and made my heart ache.

Elijah, nearly one year old and the product of rape between a fourteen-year-old girl and her step-father, was also abandoned right after birth at the hospital.

Thando, also roughly a year in age, was HIV-positive. His mother had also walked right out of the hospital doors without him.

Progress, a fourteen-month-old, with a soft head of curls, went to anyone who would pick him up. He wanted to be held at all times, and if he was put down he followed the last person who carried him around the house while he cried. He attached to anyone who would cuddle him. Progress had been found sitting next to his dead mother's body. She had died of AIDS; when a neighbor walked into the house, she found the mother dead, and Progress just sitting by her side.

Ezekiel, two years old, was missing an eye and had scars all over his bottom and legs. Scars behind his ears marked where a knife had been placed in an attempt to cut them off. His eyeball had been cut out to use as an ingredient for *muti*: medicine, or potion, for witchcraft practices.

It is believed by many South Africans that these types of concoctions, put together by a *sangoma*, or medicine man, might make a person rich, might heal a sickness, might provide whatever "miracle" the person needs. These "miracles" are advertised all over Johannesburg and the surrounding areas. People stand at the traffic lights with flyers that ask questions such as, "Want to make the love of your life fall in love with you? Need a lost love-spell caster? Want to become rich? Need a cure for AIDS?" The flyers claim that these sangomas, these traditional healers, can cast a marriage spell or a protection spell. Need revenge? They'll cast a spell. They advertise spiritual powers to accomplish anything a person might want. We Westerners wave off the flyers as they're extended to us, either because we're not into that sort of thing or we don't believe in that sort of thing. But that sort of thing isn't something to simply wave off— it's really happening. It isn't something that all people disregard as a hoax. There are many people who seek out the help of sangomas and who believe in their power, and these people will often go to great lengths for that power.

> You are the God who performs miracles;

> You display your power among the peoples.
>
> – Psalm 77:14

Where are our flyers that proclaim this truth? They can't only be in the church bulletins, handed out to the people who enter through our doors. It's on the streets where this message is needed. And I'm not talking about signs of protest and hatred that condemn sinners to hell. I'm not speaking of signs demanding repentance. I'm speaking of testifying of the love and saving power that Jesus has revealed to us. Where am I? Where are we?

Shortly after I arrived at the orphanage that day, a three-month-old, five-pound baby was dropped off by social workers. His skeleton-like arms, cone-shaped head, and sunken face revealed what the scale didn't need to. After complaints of neglect, the social

workers entered the mother's (a drug addict and prostitute) house
to find the baby soaked in his own urine, with a towel haphaz-
ardly laid over his front and back in place of a diaper. Severely
malnourished and in the advanced stages of AIDS, he seemed to
be barely hanging on. I held him like a porcelain doll, sure he
would snap in two between my arms. As I fed him his bottle, I
heard it run right through him. With the gurgling of his swollen
tummy, each suckle passed straight through his intestines and
into his diaper. I felt his clammy, delicate hands; smelt that familiar smell. . . . It was what Dad had smelled like, what his skin felt
like, right before he died.

I cuddled those children tight to my chest, praying that the love
in my heart would seep out and into theirs. I held their bottles to
their tiny mouths, made them giggle and coo, asked God to give
them all the love they'd deserved and didn't receive. These babies,
all of these babies . . . they should belong to someone who loved
them. And then I remembered: they already did. You better believe
I wanted to ask God how He loved them, because it didn't look like
He did. And then I saw the home they were at, their warms cots; I
felt my arms grow numb beneath them. Of course God loved them;
they had just had it a bit rough in this life . . . already.

By the time I walked the few footsteps back to the guest flat that
evening, I thought I'd collapse in tears; the heartache was too great.

I spent the next few weeks feeding babies, changing babies,
rocking babies, loving babies, washing laundry, cleaning up—and
then repeating it all the next day. I was being a Mom . . . all of us
volunteers were being Moms.

Then Kenton arrived. And I fell utterly in love. Kenton was
seventeen months old, and he wept unceasingly. I took him from
the social worker and laid him on the changing table to change
his nappy (what South Africans call a diaper). As I did so, I noticed
a red cord tied around his neck and another around his waist. I

asked the house-mom what it was, and she said the cords were believed to ward off evil spirits.

Some Zionists believe that a red cord, which symbolizes the blood of Christ, protects. The cords are often given by a prophet and blessed, and sometimes sprinkled with holy water. It's part of a traditional practice. I didn't know if Kenton's mother was a Zionist, if she adhered to some other traditional practices or beliefs, or if this was really what the cords were for. I didn't know his story, but I realized that someone, in the only way they knew how, wanted to protect this little boy. Which meant, deep down, that someone had loved him.

I took the scissors and cut the cords off. I prayed for Kenton, for protection over him, for him to come to know the truth of God one day, and for the blood of Jesus to cover him. He didn't need the cords, he didn't need man-made measures of safety, he just needed someone to utter Jesus over him, and to believe in the power of a prayer prayed and a savior who died and was resurrected.

Kenton continually crawled to a low window at the far end of the Haven to pull himself up and look outside. I wondered what he was looking for. Perhaps he was looking for his mom. Perhaps he was waiting for the social workers to return, or, perhaps, he was just staring out at his new surroundings. Regardless, at just under a year and half old, Kenton experienced a consuming sense of abandonment that I'd never felt in my life. At the age when he most needed his mommy, he was experiencing the loss of her. His big, dark eyes were filled with confusion and sadness. When he arrived, he couldn't walk or stand on his own yet. As his tears continued to flow, I wrapped my arms around him until he cried himself to sleep, straddled on my lap, his head resting on my chest.

Kenton's mom had also abandoned him at the crèche. Again, he'd been there a few days before he was brought to social workers and then eventually to the orphanage. I made it my goal that before I left he would be standing on his own and at least taking a few steps. We would work on it together every day.

One Saturday, on my afternoon off, a couple of volunteers and I went out for coffee. One of the girls knew of a nice little neighborhood with a coffee shop she thought we might enjoy. I had never been to this area of Johannesburg before and was completely lost. Johannesburg is a city whose population (including the surrounding suburbs) is an estimated ten million people. My hometown's population falls just short of five thousand people and the town itself, while it has a fair amount of stop signs, boasts only one traffic light—so of course I was lost. Plus, I lived in the guest flat at the orphanages and spent all my time between the home for older children and the baby orphanage, now roughly fifteen kilometers (ten miles) away.

We arrived at a quaint little place, painted an off-white, with floor-to-ceiling wood-framed windows. Maroon-colored awnings hung over the windows. To the right of the entrance were shelves of cakes, gingerbread, chocolate éclairs, baguettes, and baked goods galore. To the left of the entrance was the dining area, filled with wooden tables draped in white linen. The floor-to-ceiling windows made up two of the enclosing walls, revealing the streets and shops outside. A large, vintage chandelier hung from above, illuminating the sweets and creating a heavenly hue. Two smaller vintage chandeliers also hung inside, but their effect paled in comparison to the sun that poured in through the windows. It was a cozy, homey little hideaway, a perfect oasis for enjoying some delicious coffee and a pastry with close friends, or while reading a good story. The sign outside the entrance read, "De La Crème Cafe and Confectionery."

We chose a table right next to the windows: Amanda, Allison, Maria, and I. One friend I had met only hours earlier, and the other two only weeks before. Amanda, Maria, and I were working for orphanages. We were from different parts of the United States but there we sat in Johannesburg, South Africa, sipping coffee and enjoying our sweets, united by our love for the orphaned, the abandoned, and the neglected.

It was June 2009, during the last two weeks of my stay in South Africa. I peered out the window, wondering if I would ever set foot in this place, on this continent, again. I didn't want to leave. I dreamed about what it would be like to spend my life working with orphans, maybe even one day running my own orphanage or organization. I thought of all the babies, all the children, each with a heart-wrenching story of how they had ended up in the orphanages. Each story of a scarred past brought fresh tears to my eyes—but the unwritten stories of their futures brought hope.

Jesus loved these children. He said so in Matthew when He exclaimed, "Let the little children come to me, and do not hinder them, for the kingdom of heaven belongs to such as these." In ancient times, the little children were brought to Jesus for Him to place his hands on them and pray for them. Today, they were brought to this Christian orphanage, where we placed our hands on them and we prayed for them just as He had. We asked for more of His love so we could love more, and we kissed their cheeks and hugged them tightly. I knew in my heart that Jesus had a new story of redemption and love for each one of these children. He had a story that contained a warm home and warm arms, the love of a family, and the unconditional love of a Heavenly Father.

But, as much as I wanted to stay in this place forever, I had accepted the auditor job in Wyoming. With this commitment in mind and a dwindling bank account balance, I knew I couldn't stay here as a volunteer forever.

One morning, the sun shone in on the children's home like the glow of candlesticks, illuminating the table where twelve children and numerous aunties sat eating peanut butter porridge before Sunday service. I sat there too, gulping my porridge with the ferocity of Goldilocks, savoring each bite as I literally thought to myself, "this porridge is just right." Everything about South Africa, about Johannesburg, was just right. I sat in a state of bliss— steeping like a tea bag as I took in the richness of the culture. After all, I'd never had porridge for breakfast before. I'd only imagined its texture and taste as a little girl when Mom would recite to me the story of *The Three Little Bears*, but today even the smallest of my heart's desires was being realized.

After twelve precious tummies were filled, some of which had undoubtedly groaned for their next meal prior to their arrival at the orphanage, the aunties and I split up the children and loaded them into the cars to head to church. As I drove one of the smaller ministry cars, there was enough room for three of the children in the back and an auntie in the passenger seat. Having not yet memorized the route from the orphanage to church, I tailed Amanda, in the car ahead, with the instinct of a duckling trailing after its mother.

Amanda made a right turn, and I paused to let another car pass. Then I looked up to the top of the hill where a herd of cyclists were beginning their descent. Not wanting to allow too much distance between Amanda and myself, and thinking I had enough time before the cyclists blocked the road, I floored the gas and made a quick right turn. To my horror, I realized I had grossly miscalculated the time it would take for the cyclists to cross my path and the time it would take me to turn. I watched, with the pit of my stomach in my throat, as one cyclist tumbled off his bike and rolled. I was mortified; even though I was thankful it was the force of his brakes trying to operate at a downhill speed, as opposed to my car, that had sent him over the handle bars.

Immediately, I pulled to the side of the road and got out to apologize, and to make sure the cyclist was okay. But my apology wasn't met so well. With screaming and various choice words, I was told that I should not even be allowed to drive on the road. Unfortunately, the cyclists were right. I felt so terrible. I apologized again and got back in the car. The car door hadn't been shut a second when the kids began bouncing in their seats, one young boy's voice rising above the rest as he asked, "Auntie, Auntie. Are they going to call the police?" We prayed right then and there that they wouldn't!

I arrived at church and let out the breath I'd been holding since my close encounter with the cyclists; I never wanted to drive in Johannesburg again! In my mind, I had been inches away from killing a man. I could see it in the papers, "American charged with reckless homicide." I imagined returning to the States, only to be extradited back to South Africa for the trial. With no knowledge of the South African legal system, I dreamt up every imaginable sentence, and the bliss that had filled my mind early that morning faded with the swiftness of the flip of a switch. I shuffled the guilt around in my heart like the dragging of my high-heeled boots as I made my way into the church building. Hopeful that some worship music and the sermon would bring some encouragement, I was determined to accept the incident as simply an accident, and to be more careful in the future.

After the service, we rounded up the kids from children's church and loaded them in the car. With the kids strapped into their seatbelts in the back, I slid into the driver's seat and leaned over to place my purse underneath my feet. I had been taught that, due to the record number of hijackings in the city, I should keep my purse either in the trunk or hidden under my feet, so I performed this now routine task with efficiency. However, as I leaned down to the floor, my chest hit the horn, sounding out what I would later discover to be my mating call, HOOONNK! I quickly tried to raise my body upright in order to stop the noise, but the horn again set off a high-pitched signal: HOOONNNNNKKK!

At that exact moment, a young man who had been passing behind my car to head into the second church service assumed that I was honking at, of course, no one other than him. As he approached my car window, without rolling it down I shooed him away, motioning with my hand that I had accidentally laid on the horn. Still standing there, though, he motioned to my driver's side tire. I opened the door to find the tire to be completely flat. I hadn't noticed that!

In just one day, not only had I nearly killed someone in the ministry's car, but now I'd managed to puncture the tire. Even if I'd wanted to drive again in Jo'burg, now I doubted that I'd be allowed to!

Having spent a lot of time with Dad when he was working on our family cars, I had learned how to change a tire before I began driving. All of this previous knowledge, however, seemed to vanish completely from my mind. I took the keys in an attempt to get the spare tire out of the trunk, but between the audience of children who'd already witnessed my previous disaster and the trembling of my hands, I couldn't even manage to get the trunk opened. The young man gently took the keys from me, popped open the trunk with ease, tilted his head towards me and flashed a massive grin as if to say, "See, that was easy enough." He bent down and retrieved the spare tire, and I watched as he carried it to the driver's side to begin working. It was then that I took a hard look at him.

He had a strong, muscular build. He was a solid man, of average height, with a wide upper body. The ease in which he had lifted the spare tire out of the trunk and the bulging of his biceps proved he was accustomed to heavy lifting. His eyes were dark, so dark they nearly blended into the color of his skin, his black skin. He wasn't as dark as some South African men, though, but of a lighter complexion. His coarse hair was clipped close to his scalp. I watched his hands work. He seemed kind. I could see the kindness in his eyes, in his smile. But, after a quick perusal, my thoughts were once again turned back toward the traumatic incidents of the day.

Shortly after we discovered the flat tire, the director of the orphanage came over and instructed me to squeeze the kids, myself, and the auntie into the other cars and head back to the orphanage; she would deal with the tire and the car. With that, I ushered the kids to the other end of the parking lot. I'd taken approximately ten steps when girlish thoughts about this mystery man started emerging in my mind: "*What if this was **not** just a chance encounter, but was a serendipitous moment? And I don't even know his name!*" With that, I turned on my heels, marched back up the brick-paved parking lot, stuck my hand out and said, "I'm Holly." He looked at me a bit puzzled, flipped his hands over, mentioning how they were greasy and he wouldn't want to dirty my hands and replied, "I'm Oscar; it's nice to meet you."

I spent the next week back with the babies, loving on all of them, but especially on little Kenton as I continued to help him with his standing and walking. He was now standing on his own. He'd caught on to the fact that every time he stood for a few seconds without falling, I'd clap my hands and say, "Way to go. Ohh, good job! You're doing it!" Every time he stood, he would look straight into my eyes and immediately begin clapping his hands together. He'd clap and giggle until he'd fall back with a soft *cooosh,* his diaper bracing his fall. I'd reach for his two little hands, and he would trustingly place them in mine and let me balance him for another try.

The following Sunday, I got ready for church. That morning, due to a lack of staff, the house mom and I took two of the babies with us. One of them was Kenton. As worship began, Kenton rested on my hip and we swayed back and forth to the music. Kenton was starting to attach to me and would often look directly into my eyes, searching . . . as he murmured, "ma-ma."

It shook me to my core. "Oh baby, I'm not your mama, but I do love you," I'd reply as if he understood.

I wondered what would happen when I left. Would he feel abandoned again? Would another mama come and love him and take him home? I wanted to adopt him . . . more than the others, more than the children in India. I loved this little boy.

It was the Father's Day service and as much as Kenton was, at the moment, without an earthly father, so was I. I thought about Dad and what he'd been like. I remembered his walk and the smell of his Aspen cologne. My tears fell freely as I worshipped; three years after the death of Dad, the pain still existed. I remembered his last months as vividly as I remembered the taste of my coffee that morning. I struggled, however, to remember the sound of his voice, the feel of his hugs, and the man he was before the disease. Each year it got easier to live without him, but I imagined I would never fully stop missing him—and that was okay.

The service left me with red-rimmed eyes, a runny nose, and a heavy heart. It was my day off from the Haven, so after the service I put in my ear buds, played my iPod, and went for a walk through the suburb outside of Johannesburg where I was staying. I was so in love with Johannesburg, so blissfully happy at the orphanage, and I was content with where God had me. It was just Him and me, here in this place. I didn't have a boyfriend and though I sometimes got caught up dreaming about the man God would have for me, today, despite the sadness of not having my father, I was filled with joy about just being with God. Walking, listening to worship music—I felt like I was in the center of His will, doing exactly what I was created to do.

I busied myself until Amanda came to pick me up: we were meeting up with some friends at Mugg & Bean for evening coffee. We didn't go to the young adult evening service that day; however, we stopped at church to meet up with everyone. I had just come up the stairs to where people were exiting the service when Oscar spotted me. He locked eyes and walked directly towards me. I looked around, not knowing what to do. I was nervous. Amanda was busy talking to someone else, so I stood, paralyzed, as he approached.

"Hello, Miss Cowboy," he greeted me. (We'd had a brief conversation after the previous week's evening service, and I'd mentioned I was from rural Nebraska.) I didn't understand why he called me cowboy instead of cowgirl; maybe he was just nervous?

"Hello, Mr. Fix-It," I replied, referring to the work he'd done on my tire. *Oh gosh, this is cheesy*, I thought to myself.

"How was your week at the orphanage?" he asked.

"It was so good!" I exclaimed. "Say, we're going to Mugg & Bean, you should meet us there," and with that, Amanda came to my side and we headed back down the stairs.

When we first arrived at Mugg & Bean, there were only a few of us girls there. Shortly thereafter, the remainder of the group arrived, and in stepped Oscar. He sat directly across from me at the long table we'd all huddled around.

"Let's all share our kudos and caca from the week," Kali, one of the guys from church and Oscar's best friend, suggested.

Kudos and caca? I thought.

Everyone took turns sharing the best and the worst part of their past week, like they'd done it a hundred times before . . . the kudos and the caca.

Oscar's caca was that work was tough and he was suffering through long hours at the investment bank where he worked. My kudos was that Kenton could now stand completely on his own, while clapping his hands. Oscar and I didn't talk much directly, but just contributed to the group conversation. When everyone began filing out of the restaurant, Oscar walked alongside me.

"When do you head back to the States?" he asked.

"Wednesday," I replied.

"This Wednesday?" he questioned as I audibly felt his heart sink in his tone.

"This Wednesday."

By this time we were standing outside on the street corner. Amanda and Kali were making small talk as Oscar and I continued to shuffle our feet in an attempt to keep warm and wrap up our conversation.

"Would you be willing to have a Skype conversation with me once you get back?" he questioned.

"Sure, what's your Skype name? Will you add me?"

"I'll send you a Facebook message. Does Saturday work?"

"Sure. I'll be back on Saturday," I replied.

Oscar walked beside me all the way to Amanda's car. I looked over at him and tried to place the emotions I was feeling. I turned to him and, with a heart that was giddy and heavy all at the same time, I uttered, "Goodbye, Mr. Fix-It. It was really nice to meet you."

"Goodbye, Miss Cowboy. I will chat to you on Saturday," he replied.

Hmm, "chat to me"—that was a different way of saying it, I thought. *Must be what they say here instead of "chat with me." Either that or he thinks he's going to do all the chatting.*

I was dropped off at the airport that Wednesday evening, and I breathed in the last little bit of South Africa. Africa had already gotten into my blood—its people, its culture, its landscapes. A group of African men were playing the bongos and singing African songs right outside the departures wing. I let the music penetrate my soul.

As I passed through security and headed to my boarding gate, my eyes stopped upon a sign with a picture of the African plains and an acacia tree, with large letters which read, "This doesn't have to be your last taste of Africa." My heart leaped as if this were God's personal promise to me:

This doesn't have to be your last taste of Africa.

CHAPTER SEVEN

God's Country

I FLEW.

With emotional wings spread across the sky like the Airbus A330 I found myself in, I soared. Soared across the infinite possibilities, rose on the currents of the wind that pulled me higher. My heart surged with passion, merged into these new heights, this new level of possibility.

Swirling like the air outside the plane on the sixteen-hour-flight back to the United States, my thoughts kept returning to Oscar. *Lord, you know my heart,* I thought. *I don't want to go down the treacherous road of infatuation. I don't want to begin an emotional relationship that will only wound in the end.* As my heart expanded, it didn't see Oscar's color. I knew he was black, but for some reason, despite my previous comments as a young college girl, it no longer mattered. I was certain that if this was my Jesus-man, God would make a way. He would make a way across cultural differences, across continents, across previous expectations. I would, however, have to choose His way.

Mom picked me up from the Omaha airport late Thursday evening and we drove the familiar drive: I–80 west to Doniphan. I told her all about South Africa, all about the orphans, and all about Mr. Fix-It . . . the story of Oscar.

On June 20th, 2009 at 3 p.m. Central Time in Nebraska and 10 p.m. South African Standard Time in Johannesburg, the computer rang "doot, doot; doot doot, doot" as the Skype call flashed across my screen. My fingers shook as I clicked the lime-green Answer-With-Video button.

Oscar didn't know it, but I had only dressed fancy from the waist up. I'd tested the range of the webcam and knew it was the equivalent of a head shot, so with my hair and make-up immaculate, I didn't stress about the rest. It was summer in the States, so I wore a nice, short-sleeve red top with fluorescent yellow, Nike basketball shorts and no shoes. This was my kind of date!

I don't remember all we talked about, but I know it was about God: what He had done in our lives, what He was doing in our lives, what we dreamed He would do in our lives. I found out that Oscar had studied economics with a distinction in finance, he worked as a product control accountant at the investment bank he had talked about at Mugg & Bean, and he dreamed of traveling the world, and of changing the world.

Oscar played rugby: positions such as wing, fullback, and center, though he mostly played wing. The wings tend to attack and defend along the edges of the field, or so I learned. They must be one of the fastest and most elusive. I didn't really know the rules of rugby, though he was quick to tell me—and even quicker to let me know that in rugby they <u>don't</u> wear padding, as players do in American football!

So Oscar was accustomed to hard hits without any protection. I wanted to ask him if he was accustomed to wearing those short shorts. I'd seen pictures of rugby players, and I still couldn't understand why the shorts were so short. I reasoned, however, it was probably better just to let him continue discussing the lack of helmets, lack of padding, and the tough nature of rugby players, especially South African ones. At the end of the conversation, we prayed for each other's week and prayed for God's guidance in what was developing between us.

The morning after our first Skype conversation, I opened my inbox to find three messages from Oscar. Yes, three.

Holly, I can't stop thinking about you. Two weeks ago, my world was turned upside down and now the first thing I think about is your voice, your laugh, the way you love God, the faith you have in Him. You challenge me. I think you're beautiful, well, I know you are.

You can let me know if you will be on Skype.

Sorry for the many messages. Well, I can't stop thinking about you. You have gotten under my skin in a big way. Don't mind being a dork, because it's real. I never thought seeing you again would have this effect on me. Sorry for being forward, but it's how I feel.

When I dated in college, when I met guys in bars, at parties, I was given all these rules and tips from those around me. *Don't text him too much. Don't answer the first call and call him back. Don't always be the one to say the last thing in a text message. Don't always let him end the conversation. Don't let him know you want to see him too often.* The list of rules and game-playing went on. I'd read books on dating. Seriously. I'd even googled tips on dating; I'm not kidding. Oscar was definitely breaking the rules by sending me three messages in a row, but I didn't mind. I did decide, however, that I wouldn't go into that detail with my friends, in case they labeled him "uncool."

Every morning when I awoke, I raced down the stairs to my parents' computer room to check my messages from Oscar. It was the best alarm clock I'd ever had. I didn't have a smartphone back then, one with apps I could just roll over and bring to life. As soon as my eyes opened, I hit the floor. I took the steps four at a time, hand gliding down the railing as I swung around the corner and darted through the hallway. You can imagine what that looked like first thing in the morning, especially without the steadiness of a morning cup of coffee.

A couple of times, my early morning eyes weren't up to speed with my besotted heart, and I missed the bottom steps completely and went flying into the wall that stood in front of my parents' staircase. By reflex, my sleeping-arms would shoot to my rescue, but only to crumple against the wall a split-second before my face. (After about the third morning of catapulting head-first into the wall, I determined this was what people referred to when they talked about being "head over heels" in love.)

On the morning of the Fourth of July, our American Independence Day, I received a message from my friend Amanda from the orphanage. She asked if we could skype, and because I was up early and she late, we did. She hated to tell me what she was about to say, but Kenton had died. My heart lumped in my throat. *He was so young. He was so healthy. How?*

Kenton had awoken in the middle of the night, crying. The auntie checked on him, soothed him, and he fell back asleep. In the morning when she went to wake him, he was cold to the touch and had crusted blood running from his nose. He wasn't breathing any longer. He hadn't been breathing for some time.

Tears filled my eyes. There's no time to prepare for the sudden. Sudden loss is like leaping into the water on that first swim of summer without even dangling one's feet off the pool's edge in order to get used to the change in temperature. It's jolting and it's shocking and it often shakes our faith. There's always that temptation after loss—that temptation to stop loving as much, to stop getting as attached, because it hurts so deeply. I let the warm tears slide down my cheeks. Once again, I didn't understand. I didn't understand, but I refused to board up the walls of my heart and place a *no trespassing* sign on its entrance. God forbid I stop feeling: stop feeling the pain and become numb to it. Because in the end, if you're numb to pain it really means you're numb to a whole lot else. If a person can't feel their legs, they can't feel if you put something hot or something cold on them. They can't feel if you're pressing down firmly upon their legs or lightly touching them. If you're numb to pain, numb to hurt, you've got to be numb to joy and numb to pleasure, too. How can one go about not experiencing the negative extremes of an emotion and yet experience the positive extremes? I would feel the sorrow and I would cry; and I would continue to experience the joy of loving orphaned children—recklessly loving them. Accepting pain and accepting joy is like accepting a rose and a dandelion from the hand of a child. How could I open up my hand to accept the one from the child and yet not open up my hand to accept the other? The child's heart is unchanging even though what he presents is different. God's heart towards us is the same. In this broken world, what's presented to us is often very different from what we want, very different from what God intended when He first moved upon the face of the waters in Genesis, but His heart is unchanging. How could I look into His face and to His heart and not accept what came my way? How could I not be grateful for simply being alive—and alive enough to feel deeply?

I could accept the pain of losing Kenton and feel it, because it meant that very thing—that I had feelings. I thanked God that that little life got to experience love and laughter. I could picture Kenton standing on those golden streets in Heaven; standing on his own while he clapped and giggled uncontrollably into the face of his Heavenly Father.

> Consider it pure joy, my brothers and sisters, whenever
> you face trials of many kinds, because you know that the

testing of your faith produces perseverance. Let perseverance finish its work, so that you may be mature and complete, not lacking anything.

– James 1:2–4

Mom, Jim, and my little sister, Bailey, moved me down to
Wyoming on the Saturday, a week after the Fourth of July. We
pulled out of my parents' driveway as the morning sun settled on its
perch in the sky. The back of Jim's Chevy pick-up truck was jammed
full of my belongings, as was the trailer we'd hitched to it. We were
headed even further west, to move me into my new home.

I watched the endless sea of corn-fields and pasture land, the
prominent geography of western Nebraska, pass by the back seat
window of Jim's Chevy, where I was packed into the backseat with
Bailey. The corn should be knee high or even taller by the Fourth
of July; at least that's what they say in my hometown. Whenever
July rolls around, so does the saying, "The corn should be knee-
high: knee-high by the Fourth of July." Then talk of whether the
corn is knee-high or taller that year occurs, and what have been
the contributing factors. Lots of rain, not enough rain, etc.

Once you've driven past Ogallala and further west, the radio
station selection gets pretty slim. We didn't have XM radio and
Jim loves old western music. Bailey, who was twelve years old at
the time, had her Ipod so loud that her Kidz Bop (or whatever it
was) was mixing with the western music in the backseat, creating
a musical style I didn't think had been heard before.

A large sign, showcasing a beautiful picture of the Rocky
Mountains and a cowboy riding a bucking bronco with "Welcome
To Wyoming—Forever West" written in large yellow letters
across it, welcomed us across the state line. Roughly five hours
and 350 miles later, we took the exit 362 off ramp and pulled into
Cheyenne. Wyoming is often called "God's country" because of

its stunning scenery and the vastness of its undeveloped and untouched land. I was about to be dropped off in God's country . . . forever west . . . all alone.

I inspected my new town as we drove to find my apartment. I'd picked a charming little one-room apartment in an attractive building with a cream-colored exterior and rustic red shingles on the roof. The wooden balconies sat like flower boxes outside the sliding glass doors and served as awnings for the patios below. I liked my apartment, but I was unsure how I felt about this new season, about this new town, and about being all alone. I knew no one in Cheyenne; I had no family there, no friends. I felt as though I was being dropped off in the middle of a desert.

I set my mind to the task of unpacking. By the end of the evening, we managed to have everything unloaded from the pick-up truck and trailer, so we ordered pizza and settled in. I didn't want my family to leave in the morning. And as much as I knew that Bailey was glad to finally have me out of the house again, I was going to miss her.

Jim was up early, ready to get back on the road. We ate a sunrise breakfast together at McDonald's and then they dropped me back off at my apartment. I hugged Mom, Jim, and Bailey. I didn't want to let them go; I didn't want them to leave me here. I stood on the pavement near the curb of the street, tears streaming down my cheeks as I waved goodbye and watched the pick-up pull away. This was it. Mom said I was a big girl now. But was I really? I felt so small, so alone, so much like a child in a big and scary, unknown world. But, this was my new life.

I walked back inside my apartment and took a look at the boxes stacked and strewn from room to room. I had a lot of work to do, and yet, I didn't want to do a thing. Before unpacking, I decided to head to Wal-Mart to get some cleaning supplies, nails, lining paper for the cupboards, and a few other items. I stood in front of the bathroom mirror, pulled my hair back in a ponytail and tied a red bandana around it. I rarely wore bandanas, but thought it an appropriate apparel item considering my day would be dedicated to cleaning and unpacking. As I brushed the mascara onto my eyelashes, I paused in the mirror, wishing I had looked up a church before I arrived. It was early Sunday morning and as much as I needed to get things sorted around the house, I wanted to go to church. I knew it was going to be a difficult transition and the sooner I found a church, the better.

Before coming to Cheyenne, I had prayed some crazy prayers. I like to ask God to go ahead and be radical; I told him I was willing if He was willing. I prayed that the first people I met would be people that would become my friends. I prayed that the first church I went to would be my church. I prayed that all the firsts would just *be*. Maybe I was lazy and didn't want to have to try too hard to make friends, try too hard to settle in, or try too hard to establish, but I figured I'd pray the prayers anyway.

Wal-Mart was just a couple of miles down the road from my apartment. As I was pulling into the parking lot, I noticed a homeless gentleman, apparently in his mid-forties, with unbrushed hair and unwashed clothes sitting near the stop sign. I hadn't thought there would be many homeless people around these parts. As I drove past, I felt God whisper to my heart, "Go buy him breakfast." I looked around and saw a McDonald's inside of Wal-Mart, so I reasoned that after I'd bought all of my supplies I would grab breakfast on my way out of the store. It had been about thirty minutes when I finally reached the counter at McDonald's. Unsure of what this man might like for breakfast, I decided to order two sausage McGriddle meals with two cups of orange juice and two coffees. Maybe he needed both to drink. Maybe I needed to have breakfast again too, I reasoned, since at my first breakfast I hadn't eaten much.

I loaded everything into my car and began driving to the stop sign. As I approached where I had seen him, I noticed he was no longer there, but had begun walking and was about fifty yards away. I threw my car into park, jumped out without even shutting the door or turning the car off, and began jogging and yelling, "Sir, Sir. I have your breakfast."

I was clearly aware that I was chasing down a homeless man. I was also clearly aware that this might give my parents a heart attack. The man stopped and began walking in my direction. I handed him his breakfast and we began talking. He told me he had been picked up by a couple and brought to a church function the night before, and they had invited him back to church this morning. He asked me for the time: the Sunday school started at 9:45 a.m. and church at 11:00 a.m. We could still make it, and he asked if I would give him a ride; he was pretty sure he remembered the way to the church and could get us back there.

There was a brief moment when I remembered Mom's words, her advice as I was growing up: "It's okay to give to the homeless, but it's not safe to pick them up or give them rides if you're alone or alone with children."

But I reasoned that I wasn't alone, because God was with me. So with that, I invited Joe, a once nameless homeless man, and now no longer a stranger, into my car. We would find this church and I would not only drop him off, but I would go with him. After all, had I not, just a few moments before, sent up a wishful prayer about wanting to go to church?

After a few wrong turns, we made it to a modest-sized Baptist church on Sunflower Road. Only a few cars were parked out front and in the gravel parking lot. We were about thirty minutes early for Sunday school, but Joe insisted we could go inside and eat our breakfast. So, with that, Joe and I entered the little church, greeted the pastor, who remembered Joe, and were directed to the kitchen to eat our McDonald's.

As we unwrapped our McGriddles and gulped our coffee, Joe told me about his life. He had been adopted as a child, but at the age of fifteen had run away from home. He had been in and out of jail for domestic violence, had lived on and off the streets, and was now trying to make his way to Washington state, where he wanted to take care of a warrant for his arrest. He was going to try to get things straightened out.

Life had been hard on Joe and, though he knew about Jesus, Joe had often turned his back on Him. I shared a little bit about my life too, and then began telling Joe what a blessing he, Joe, had been to me. I shared with him that earlier in the morning I had wanted to come to church and that it wasn't really *me* who had brought him, but *he* had brought me! God had used Joe to answer my prayer.

Had I not listened to that prompting and bought him breakfast, I don't believe I would have gone to church that day. I believe that God would have brought me to the church even if I hadn't bought Joe breakfast. However, I also believe that because that couple and I had listened to the voice of God and obeyed Him, a more beautiful and more powerful testimony was revealed. The chain reaction that can occur when individuals obey the promptings of God is supernatural; and it brings God glory—so much more glory!

Some people disagree with giving money or food to beggars. Some people believe that it only perpetuates the problems of poverty, and that "a handout always keeps a hand out." I'm certain many charitable organizations can prove this very fact. I do believe that this often is the case, and that a handout often does keep a hand out. Some people argue that giving money or food to the poor creates laziness and dependency. And, I agree. It sometimes does. *Sometimes.* But if someone is lazy, I want to love them to the point that I can introduce them to the One who says *look to the ant and consider its ways and be wise* (Proverbs 6:6). I'm going to choose, however, not to call them a sluggard. I by no means want to perpetuate poverty and laziness. However, I also believe that extending a hand to the hands of the poor often provides an open door for us to tell them about the One who can provide hope despite their poverty, to tell them about the One who can help break its cycle, and to help change their mindsets. When God commanded us to care for the poor, the widow, and the orphan, He didn't put a disclaimer there that says "do not feed or give to beggars, because it only perpetuates the problem." God said, "He that hath pity upon the poor lendeth unto the Lord; and that which he hath given will He pay him again" (Proverbs 19:17 KJV). So who are we to say that poverty will be perpetuated by our act? Maybe for one beggar it will. But, for another, maybe it won't. Which one do we choose to see? And what if we're wrong? Can we not see the one—the one placed in front of us? Who are we to look among all the beggars and label them drunk or lazy? And who are we to judge the impact of our giving? The Hebrew word for "given" in the above scripture—"and that which he hath given"—is *gemul.* In Hebrew, this word was used to describe the dealing out of punishment or the dealing out of a reward. It more literally means "the dealing of the hands or of one's hands." It is a reward or punishment dealt by the hands. May I keep my hands out, may we keep our hands out, and let people know that when they come in contact with us, they can keep their hands out. We're not always called to give them food or clothes or money, but we can take their hands in ours and we can bow our heads and pray together. We can always bow our heads.

One of the directors of the orphanages in South Africa (who I worked with later) taught me that we should always leave something behind. Yes, we may get taken advantage of. Yes, we should protect ourselves and use our judgment, but we should practice the act of leaving something behind. He tells the story from Ruth chapter two, where Ruth is gleaning grain from Boaz's fields. Boaz commands his workers to leave some bundles of grain behind for her to gather, and to also pull some heads of grain from their bundles and leave them for her. God commanded in the Law, "When you reap the harvest of your land, do not reap to the very edges of your field or gather gleanings of your harvest. Leave them for the poor and for the foreigner residing among you. I am the Lord your God" (Leviticus 23:22).

Remembering that command and that story, this director's wife always has a bag of oranges in her car. At every traffic light she stops at, if there is a beggar, she hands the beggar an orange—regardless. She is always leaving something behind. She doesn't stop to remember the scripture and say to herself, "Well, Ruth was working and this man isn't." She doesn't stop to question whether she's doing more harm than good—she just does what is good in that moment: providing food to someone who needs it. I want to be a person who always leaves something behind. And I want you to be that kind of person, too. I don't want us to depend on government systems or fight over the reallocation of wealth; I don't want us to have to reallocate our wealth. I want us to share and give, because God asks us to. Some people will always be wealthier than others, and I believe that is okay. Jesus said the poor will always be among us (John 12:8). But I want us each to live to be a blessing and to believe that God will bless us—based on His definition of blessing, whether it is physical or spiritual. Blessed to be a blessing.

So God had asked me, in faith, to bless Joe with breakfast, so that God, in turn, could bless me with a church. And even if God hadn't had a physical blessing for me to reap, I was still called to bless.

As people filed in for church, Joe and I took a seat in side-by-side, mauve-cushioned chairs which connected to form a back-row pew. About forty people, conservatively and nicely dressed, found their seats. I looked around, and then down at my own clothes for the first time. I had forgotten that I hadn't really dressed for church. With a red bandana, an *I love New York* t-shirt, black basketball shorts, and flip-flops that revealed the tattoo on my foot, I imagined the others thought I was a heathen. Joe, with unwashed clothes and unbrushed hair, didn't necessarily look any better.

We definitely looked out of place, but I imagined that Jesus was smiling. He had always welcomed those who didn't look the part. Surely, God's heart was overjoyed by the fact that Joe, His son, was in His house today. *Welcome home, Joe;* that's what God would be saying. Even if it would be a long time before Joe was in church again, I imagined it pleased Jesus. I imagined there was more rejoicing in Heaven that day, because of Joe, than because of the rest of us who filled those cushioned seats.

The church service was much different than what I was used to. I normally attended a non-denominational church, with a loud band, charismatic worship, and a forty-five-minute to an hour-long message. At this little Baptist church, we opened hymnals to classic hymns as a lone piano blended with our voices. I remembered some of these songs from the years I'd spent as a child at the Lutheran church in my hometown. I let the poetic melodies drift off my lips and into the sanctuary, imagining them swirling before the throne of God. Despite how different this church was from what I was used to, I felt like this was exactly where God wanted me to be during my time in Cheyenne.

At first, I daydreamed with my pride. I began thinking about how I could help paint the walls, maybe invite other individuals my age to church, and get a band going. I could be so good for this church; add so much; bring so much to help it grow. When God brings us to a place or introduces us to a person, it never ceases to amaze me how we often begin to walk through all the ways in which we can impact or change that place or person to fit our ideas. Instead, we should be opening ourselves up to how God might want a particular place or individual to change us and shape us.

It took a while for me to hear Him, but God spoke these words directly to my heart: He hadn't brought me to this little church to change it or make it like my home church: He had brought me to this church so through it He could change *me*, shape *me* . . . so He could grow me. So I didn't invite anyone my age to the church. The walls did get repainted, but not by me. I didn't start a huge band. We continued to sing along with the accompaniment of one piano, sometimes one guitar. I learned scripture. I was taught scripture. And, I grew in my understanding of the Bible and of the context and culture in which it was written. There were some stances taken on the interpretation of scripture that I didn't agree with, and I asked God to continually challenge my thinking and show me if and when I might be misguided. Despite that, I believed this was where God had me for a reason and for a season. I grew in simplicity and in modesty. I spent much of my season at the church on my knees, praying for God to clothe me in humility and righteousness.

> All of you, clothe yourselves with humility toward one an-
> other, because "God opposes the proud, but shows favor to
> the humble."
>
> – 1 Peter 5:5

If there's one thing I've found that God tries to cast out of us immediately, it's pride. Unfortunately, I've also found that if there's anything that tries to continually fight itself back into our hearts, it's pride. I have to make a conscious choice, daily, to humble myself, and to see myself as a valuable and useful tool of God's, but not a necessary tool. When surrendered, He will use me abundantly to accomplish His will, but He is totally capable of accomplishing His will without me. The more I choose to see my ideas as expressions of His creativeness and my successes as expressions of His grace, the more He wins the battle against pride in my heart.

After that first church service, I couldn't contain myself. I couldn't wait to get home and skype with Oscar; to tell him all that God had done. He was the first person I wanted to tell. Oscar listened in awe as

I recounted the day's events. He listened to me and rejoiced with me. I liked that. I liked having someone who also saw the hand of God in everything and got just as delighted as I did.

I don't know what happened to Joe. I dropped him off at a truck stop near the interstate, so he could hitch a ride to Washington. The thought of driving him to Washington did cross my mind (I had family there), but I would be starting work soon and I didn't have a lot of money. Plus, I thought that might have been considerably unwise. I like to believe that Joe made it to Washington and served his time in jail. I like to believe he is out there somewhere, living a life devoted to Jesus and ministering to others who are in the position he once was. I hope one day I get to see him again, and that I recognize him. And, I hope I get to tell him one more time that when he brought me to Faith Baptist Church, he was assisting God in changing me, because God didn't just change my life; He changed me. And in changing me, He did more than just change my life.

Just a few days later, Oscar asked me to date him with the intention of marriage: he was very clear about his intentions. I said yes. Well, at first I actually told him I needed to pray about it one more time. He got a bit despondent as he ended the Skype call to go to sleep. I told him that my delay wasn't a *no*, I just wanted to pray about it, and I would give him my answer the next day. In every way, I wanted to say *yes* immediately. There was something inside of me, however, that knew that if I said yes I was saying yes for the rest of my life; and that was scary for me. I knew I wouldn't only be saying yes to date him, but also to marry him. Oscar wasn't asking me to marry him yet, he was simply stating that his intention was marriage. But, this yes was bigger for me. I had to be certain.

I remembered writing a quote in my journal when I was in India. It stated, "A man is like a river: he either takes you closer to God or he takes you farther from Him. The man you marry should be carrying you closer to the Father."

I thought about this quote and about Oscar. In every way, he was drawing me closer to the Father's heart. I also thought about another quote that I'd written—not in my journal, but on my heart, long ago. I'd never really lived by it in the past, but I decided it was a good time to start. It reads, "A woman's heart should be so wrapped up in Christ that a man must be seeking the Lord to find it." I continued to wrap my heart up in Christ, and Oscar continued to find it. It was in both of us seeking God's heart that we began to find each other's.

When Oscar phoned me back I said yes. I would date him with the intention of marriage. And, I couldn't be more thrilled. He breathed a sigh of relief and then grinned from ear to ear. He couldn't believe that I hadn't said yes immediately. I mean, how could I have not said yes to him immediately? His smile continued to dimple his cheeks; and mine did the same. We sat there, staring into each other's eyes through the computer screen, grinning into our web cameras. Him on one continent and me on another, and our smiles the curved bridge in between.

CHAPTER EIGHT

The Desert

I CRIED.

Tears of loneliness and discouragement found their way out of my heart often in Wyoming. But frequent tears had been finding their way to my face for a couple of years now. I wondered if I might have a problem other than depression, like some incessant crying disorder. Or maybe it was just all the changes. Maybe, it was because my boyfriend was on the other side of the planet. Whatever it was, crying in Wyoming felt worse, because no matter how hard I cried, no one was there to see or give me sympathy. It was one of those times when the only person who really knew was Jesus.

When I was in South Africa, one of the volunteers I had worked with told me she felt that I was a flower whom God was going to pluck up and re-plant in the middle of a desert—but in that desert I would begin to bloom and blossom. She went on to tell me that one doesn't typically think of a flower being uprooted and planted in the desert only to begin blooming and blossoming, but she felt that was just what God was going to do with me.

I wonder if that's what he does with a lot of us. When we're feeling the heat, feeling the dryness, do we just need to remember that we're still flowers; even though it feels like we're in the desert? Deserts do actually host a number of beautiful flowers and plants. These plants have adapted to the extremes of the heat and dryness by adapting both physically and behaviorally. Some plants, such as cacti, adapt their physical structure by having few leaves and storing large amounts of water. Others grow extremely long roots, allowing them to obtain water from at or near the water table. Could that be what God was doing—deepening my roots? Could that be what He's doing when we're feeling dry—deepening our roots, so we can reach more of Him? So we don't have to wait for the sporadic or seasonal showers, but we can learn to reach down to the water table?

> But whoever drinks the water I give them will never thirst. Indeed, the water I give them will become in them a spring of water welling up to eternal life.
>
> – John 4:14

I thought my blossoming might be the purpose of my tears, that I'd water that desert into some fertile land. I didn't know, but I just kept crying. I wanted to board a plane and head back to South Africa to hold abandoned babies, to hold the hand of my precious man. Instead, I boarded myself into my black suit, held my computer bag in one hand, clenched my coffee mug in the other, and headed down the career path of an audit associate.

In the auditing industry, the motto for first year associates is "sink or swim." You are thrown in deep, and the learning curve is steep; you either choose to swim or you sink beneath the audit files, the work papers, the never-ending adjusting journal entries, the page after page of review comments. I thought I might drown in my own tears before I sank, though.

One night in my apartment, as I'd finished a bubble bath, lit some candles, and crawled beneath my suede duvet, I opened the bookmarked pages in a book I was reading and came across some powerful scriptures. Hosea 2:14-15 reads, "Therefore, I am now going to allure her, I will lead her into the desert and speak tenderly to her heart. There I will give her back her vineyards, and will make the valley of Achor a door of hope. There she will sing as in the days of her youth, as in the days she came up out of Egypt."

In the Bible, the valley of Achor was a valley near Jericho. *Achor* means "trouble" in Hebrew, so this valley is literally "the valley of trouble." Joshua 7:10–26 says it was the place where Achan was stoned for breaking God's commands. It was in that valley where trouble was brought on the Israelite camp because of the sin of Achan and his wife. When God says He will make the valley of trouble a door of hope, He is saying that though we deserve trouble and destitution for our sin, He will take that trouble and make it a doorway for hope. He took that trouble upon Himself as His Son did, and because of that we've got hope . . . a doorway of hope. With Jesus, we don't have the same fate as Achan and his wife did. That's what He was showing us; that's what He was showing me. We can sing as in the days of our youth. He had to allure me to that desert place, to that place where it was dry and lonely, where sin no longer satisfied me, so I might want more of Him. He brought me to Himself.

Oscar and I skyped every day while I was in Wyoming. He would wake up at 5 a.m. South African time so he could talk to me before he went to work, and I would stay up late every night so I could talk to him before I went to sleep. One night he indicated that, since our relationship was progressing, there was one thing in particular he wanted to discuss.

"Since we're dating with the intent of possibly getting married, Hols, there's something I want to share with you," Oscar stated.

My heart quickened.

"I may have been a bit rebellious in my past . . . partying and kissing too many girls, . . . but . . . " Oscar continued.

All I could think was, oh no! He was directing the conversation to the topic of sex and then he was going to ask . . . he was going to ask me if I had waited.

"I'm saving myself for my wife, Hols. I haven't slept with anyone; I'm a virgin," he said, as embarrassment flashed across his face. "It's the gift I want to give to my wife on our wedding night. The best gift of all—myself completely." And then, he stared back into the webcam, straight into my eyes, waiting. He was waiting for me to say something, anything. The realization of what I had done split my heart in two as I realized I was about to break his.

"I am so sorry!" I said.

Oscar looked at me for more explanation, not saying a word. Hurt surfaced in his eyes.

"How many?"

I held my hand up, fingers to the webcam, reflecting what I couldn't say. His head lowered as he nodded.

"I need to leave for work now, Hols," Oscar's voice trailed off. "I'll talk to you later."

The Skype call ended and I burst into tears. Again! Tears waterlogged my pillow that night, as I wondered if Oscar would change his mind about me. The actions of my past flooded back, reminding me of all I'd done. I felt condemned, even though I knew God said there was no condemnation in Him. I hadn't grown up surrounded by a lot of men who thought the way Oscar did, so I never imagined that a man would truly wait to give himself until marriage. And even though my parents, with pointed finger, had said "no sex until marriage," I had decided one night in middle school that if I waited until I was sixteen, that was probably good enough.

I awoke the following morning with a mascara-blotched pillow and a message from Oscar. I wasn't sure I wanted to click the "Open Message" button.

I read:

"Who is she? She is not her past. She is worthy. She does not have to earn my heart. She does not have to earn my respect. She is God's dear little girl: pure in His eyes, strong, and worthy of a real man. A man who is seeking after God's heart. She is my queen, perfect as she is. Her past does not make her less beautiful to me. She is now God's perfect little girl. She is my gift. Her heart is my gift. She is the woman I am falling for, falling in love with. She is my girlfriend. She has my heart. She has my trust, she is my love. I still want to hold her, I still desire to kiss her. She is my lioness. My queen. My love. Rise, my queen, for your king wants you by his side. Rise, my queen. Forget what is behind you and look to what is in front of you. Rise, Holly."

My heart gasped. This was a man's heart toward me? This was Oscar's heart towards me! And more important, this was God's heart towards me. I saw it in those words.

Oscar was an image, in the flesh, of how God loved me, though I knew that God's love was a perfect love, a deeper, more unconditional love. Oscar allowed me to see a picture of my relationship with Jesus, teaching me what it means to experience the love of Christ in human form. He was my Jesus-man. God showed me that day what true redemption felt like. I still battled with condemnation and guilt from my past, but God gently reminded me again and again: "there is no condemnation for those who are in Christ Jesus" (Romans 8:1).

Oscar and I continued to skype every day for an hour before he went to work and for an hour before I went to sleep. I then spent most Saturday mornings having Skype dates with him. I'd pour myself a cup of coffee, he would have his cup of tea, and we'd talk just as if we were right across the table from one another. Oscar told me stories of his life, about growing up in a village, how he obtained his education.

Oscar had a thick South African accent, one I was told was influenced by the all-boys school he attended growing up. He pronounced his words much like the British. He used the word *must* a lot, saying things like "we must go to the movie when I arrive." When he pronounced the word *literally*, it sounded more like *litrly*.

Sometimes I had to listen very carefully in order to pick up certain words. Oscar was always saying "pardon," or "pardon me." If I thanked him for something, he replied, "pleasure," or "it's a pleasure." I loved that. When he talked of time going by fast, he didn't draw out his *a*, but pronounced it with a short vowel: "time is going by fahst." Sometimes I'd close my eyes and just listen to his voice. It was musical.

Oscar told me about his parents. They grew up under apartheid in South Africa. Apartheid was a system of racial segregation, similar to segregation in the United States, which lasted from 1948 until 1994. His parents, though they had homes of their own in the villages they grew up in, had traveled to Johannesburg when they were young to find work, and they had always worked for white families. This made me nervous. I was white. My skin color matched the skin color of those whom his parents had served. So I wasn't sure they would fully accept me. If they did accept me, would they think I would expect preferential treatment, or to be waited on? Deep down, would they always wish I was a woman from their own culture? Or not necessarily their own culture, but a black woman, at least?

Oscar, born in 1983, grew up during the last years of apartheid, but he felt sheltered from a lot of what was going on around him. His only memory of the direct effects of that time, one he still carried with him, occurred when he was about nine years old.

As he sat outside a shop one day, in the back seat of his father's employer's car, he had waved excitedly at the young white couple who were parked one space over. Growing tired of Oscar's frantic waving, the young woman looked directly at him: "you're black, *and* you're irritating," she pronounced. Oscar stopped waving, dropped his hand, and turned his head sadly away, understanding the fullness of what this white woman was saying to him—and about him.

But Oscar didn't stereotype people based on the color of their skin, or lump everyone who was white into the category: "People Who Hate Me." He'd grown up with his father's employers loving him and treating him like one of their own children. The white family that Oscar's father worked for paid for Oscar's entire education. They paid for him to go to a semi-private school and even paid for him to attend college. When Oscar was young, it was the daughter of this family who gave him his very first Bible.

Oscar experienced unconditional love at the hands of white people, so even when words or looks of hate were thrown his way, he never thought something was wrong with him. He just thought the people being hateful were mean, because he knew a white family and white people who treated him with a lot of love. A white family had reached out and dramatically impacted Oscar's life, and that impact birthed a passion inside Oscar to one day be able himself to significantly impact other people's lives. Those acts of kindness and generosity to one child had started a chain reaction—a chain reaction of God's glory and love.

I couldn't imagine what it must have felt like to be hated because of the color of your skin. I'd never experienced hatred because of my skin color. I'd never been told that I was irritating just because I was a certain color. In my small rural community, almost everyone was either white or Hispanic. Growing up, there were only a couple of black families in our town, and by the time I was eleven or twelve they had moved away. Growing up, I had known that cultural differences existed, but I never once thought that one race was superior to another or that everyone didn't deserve the same amount of respect. Some people I knew, and many people I grew up around, had other ideas about skin color, however. So I knew that a lot of people around me would be both shocked and appalled to learn that I was dating a black man.

I didn't care.

I thought I would care. I'd always been overly concerned with what people thought about me, or if they were talking behind my back. This time, I knew some were talking behind my back, and I simply didn't care. The evening before I'd left Johannesburg, I was walking through a shopping mall with a friend when I noticed a biracial couple in front of me. I looked down to see them holding hands: that picture of intertwined black and white hands was etched upon my heart. At that moment, I felt God whisper to my heart: *You have one master—and no other.* So I knew I wasn't supposed to try to please everyone. I wasn't to be afraid of what people would say when I came back from South Africa and told them I liked a black man. I was supposed to listen to my one Master, to listen only to what *He* said.

Each time I went back to Nebraska to visit my family, my stepdad, Jim, was mentioning a different nice young man he knew. One night, we all went out for pizza and one of the long-haul truckers Jim knew "just happened" to meet us at the restaurant. He was a bit older than me, and I was a bit confused as to why he was there. (I remember that night because it was the night Bailey accidently shaved half her eyebrow off trying to use Mom's eyebrow trimmer. I couldn't stop laughing. Mom had even tried to pencil the shaved half back in, but it just looked worse. Bailey has dark eyebrows, and she was in middle school: at that phase in her life when *everything* mattered and *everything* was one hundred times worse than it actually was. So she got angry about all the laughter. But the angrier she got, the more her brow furrowed. The more her brow furrowed, the more those pencil marks creased and bobbed, and the more we laughed; and the more unbearable it became for poor Bailey.)

Jim kept trying to introduce me to different men, because he was leery about this black man from Africa I had come home talking about. Jim had never thought his step-daughter would bring home a black man; he'd grown up seeing inter-racial marriage, but he never thought it would affect his family. If Oscar and I got married, our children would be neither black nor white: would they be accepted? Jim thought hard about the challenges that children of mixed race face: feeling like they might not really fit in, either in the white community or the black community. These would be his grandchildren, and he was concerned they might feel that they never fit in anywhere.

But I kept ignoring Jim's semi-introductions to these different men. Growing up, I'd heard people comment that God said to marry within your tribe and that inter-racial marriage wasn't biblical. I thought about that. I thought about that real hard, and then I read those scriptures. I read those scriptures in the Old Testament where God disapproves of men bringing home foreign wives, where He tells the Israelites to marry within their culture. I read them and I understood them.

God's words had nothing to do with the foreignness or the race of those women. Foreign women—and men, for that matter—worshipped foreign gods. They worshipped Baal, and they sacrificed children in fire to Molech. They had orgies under trees as worship to the fertility gods. So God wanted the Israelites to marry only other Jews *not* because He was against inter-racial marriage, but because He didn't want them to fall into idol worship and so fall away from Him. It happened all the time when a man took a foreign wife: soon the man would be building altars and offering sacrifices to other gods. Even kings, the leaders of the nation, did this! And this angered God. And it grieved God. God wasn't and isn't concerned about the color of an individual's skin, but rather the condition of their heart. Skin color is just the package that wraps up that heart, and that heart's condition can be good or it can be bad, regardless of the looks of that outer packaging.

⌒ ⌒

Despite feeling like I was in the desert, and was ready to leave Wyoming and head straight back to South Africa, I did blossom. I didn't sink at work and, though the learning curve was steep, I continued to progress. I was by no means the most intelligent first year associate, neither did I understand everything. I made mistakes and I followed prior year working papers too closely, without applying my brain, but I was willing to learn and to stay positive. I traveled across Wyoming on various audits with my audit teams; to Laramie, to Casper, to Rock Springs, to Cody, to Powell; all across God's country and into Colorado. We often spent a week at a time in hotels, and I loved the traveling and seeing the new places. Some were small towns, with one main road and a population no bigger than my hometown. Others were larger, with breathtaking landscapes and mountain views. I might not be flying across countries, but I was getting to explore a state, a countryside. I was in God's country and I was getting to know this God of mine even more.

I spent most of my time alone: reading books, reading the Bible, going for long walks on Cheyenne's walking and bike trail that forged its way through the city. I would stop in at the gas station down my street and get a cappuccino, turn on my car's stereo and just drive: drive through the countryside, entranced by the open plains, the long prairie grass. God was speaking tenderly to my heart and I was becoming a whole person—in Him. There were times when I didn't know if I could bear it, but God always tenderly reminded me that I wasn't alone. "Have I not commanded you? Be strong and courageous. Do not be afraid, do not be discouraged, for the Lord your God will be with you wherever you go" (Joshua 1:9).

God had introduced me to the love of my life, but Oscar was not going to make me complete; he was not my other half. God intended for us to be two whole people coming together, so God was busy making me whole in Him, and in Him alone. I was falling in love with Oscar, but I was falling in love with God too—even more.

"My queen, it is done," Oscar beamed back at me on Skype one evening. "I have bought my tickets to the States and I will arrive in December." Oscar had long ago begun calling me "my queen." I never fought the nickname; what woman would? Oscar was coming to spend Christmas in the States, to spend it with me, and to meet my family . . . to meet my family.

I got to the airport four hours early. I wanted to be sure I was in the arrivals area when Oscar disembarked from his flight. I'd bought a whole new outfit. And I'd bought new perfume. I was so nervous my stomach was queasy. I got a coffee at the airport and sat on the bench, waiting. When the coffee hit my stomach, causing a nuclear reaction, I realized it was too strong. I called my friend and told her I felt like the volcano science experiment, when baking soda and vinegar are combined and erupt like lava out of a *paper-mache* volcano. I told her this day wasn't going as planned. She didn't offer any comfort, but instead laughed in my ear so hard I decided I'd just find something else to do while I waited.

I paced from the arrivals area to the flight board, checking the status of Oscar's flight. A huge Christmas tree dotted with red poinsettias stood in the center of the Denver arrivals area. I stared at that tree for a long time. I love Christmas time. Not for the presents, but for the presence: the presence of people, the presence of family. I watched military men walk up the escalators in their camouflage uniforms and army boots. I watched them embraced tighter than those boots were laced. My eyes got all teary. I watched grandmas hug grandchildren, wives wrap arms around husbands, their child in the middle. Then I stood up and inched closer. I inched closer, because it was time. Oscar's flight had landed, and any minute he would rise into view on those escalators. Ascending to me.

My head ducked and swerved as clusters of people began to flow off the escalator. I couldn't miss him. My heart stopped every time a new cluster appeared. Was he in this group? Where was he? And then, I saw him.

He was wearing a dark blue, winter jacket, Timberland boots, and the largest smile I'd ever seen. I was wearing one too. He looked like a clown on freeze-frame; I smiled until my cheeks hurt, and then smiled some more.

I didn't know how long I should hug him. Surely, I should hug him. I mean shaking his hand would be weird. I hadn't been around him physically when he was my boyfriend though, so it was awkward.

"Hello, my queen," Oscar said in a slow voice, beaming at me the whole time.

"Hi," I jittered.

We hugged for an appropriate amount of time. I thought it might be like one of those military men embraces, but we weren't there yet. His head went right, left, mine went right, left and then we just kind of loosely opened our arms and squeezed a little. It wasn't like I'd seen in the movies, but I didn't get too disappointed. It was, after all, our first hug.

Oscar and I held hands for a moment while we were walking through the airport to collect his bags. But not long after, he let my hand go. We both kept looking around. It was somewhat uncomfortable for him. It was somewhat uncomfortable for me. We wondered what people might be thinking. Would they be thinking anything? He said if we were in South Africa, in his country, he would feel at ease. Here, he felt nervous: as if we were being scandalous, or doing something wrong. Because he didn't see as many black people as he was used to, Oscar was self-conscious. Holding hands for the first time, and for the first time in public, was hard. We didn't feel uncomfortable holding hands because we were embarrassed of one another. We felt uncomfortable because we feared that someone might actually say something mean and nasty or give us a dirty look. We weren't prepared to handle reactions—good or bad. It was all so new; so unexpected.

Oscar had wanted to try Burger King for a long time. There was a Burger King in the airport, so I took him there. We didn't consider this our first date, just grabbing a bite before we hit the road. I ordered a chicken sandwich: you know, the one with the creamy mayonnaise and lettuce. I was hungry because all I'd had was that toxic coffee, but I pretended as if I wasn't. I wanted to eat my entire sandwich, but instead I left a third of it on the crumbled wrapper, thinking this was a good first impression. I threw a couple of words out like, "oh boy, I'm full" as I played with my half-eaten fries. I was not full.

We loaded his suitcases in the car and began the drive from Denver to Cheyenne. I had blown up an air mattress in my front living room, and we'd stay the night at my apartment and leave for my parents' place in Nebraska the next morning. It was dark and had been snowing. I veered onto I–25 north, to Cheyenne. It was icy and cold; I drove a slow forty miles an hour, because if I drove any faster my car started to slide.

"Maybe we should pray," I quickly glanced over at Oscar.

Oscar said a prayer for safety and I slowed the car even more. The windshield wipers frantically swept the wet, heavy, falling snow. Oscar had seen snow for the first time when he'd landed in

New York, just prior to flying to Denver. But he hadn't seen driving in snow. I leaned on the steering wheel, inching my face closer to the windshield.

My car began to slide. I let off the gas and gripped the wheel as we began spinning. We spun out of the right-hand lane and into the middle of the interstate. In slow motion I watched as the median came into view, then the ditch on the right side, and the median again. In the center of both lanes, we circled once, circled twice, circled a third time.

CHAPTER NINE

Itsomi Yo Busikha

WE SPUN.

"Stay calm, stay calm," Oscar's voice circled with the car. We slid to a stop just off the side of the road, back in the right-hand lane, facing the correct direction. It was as if we hadn't spun at all and I'd just pulled off onto the side of the road. My hands were trembling, though, and my legs shook. A car passed us. Had it come moments earlier, it could have slammed into us as we spun. Oscar hugged me from across the seat: "You did great!"

"That was scary," I replied; "I didn't know what to do." I hadn't known what to do, but I'd always been told if that happened I shouldn't try to overcorrect or oversteer, so I just kept my hands on the wheel like normal, all the while repeating "Lord. Lord. Lord."

We had no trouble driving out of the snow on the shoulder, so I just drove right on as if nothing had happened. I'd driven in snow my whole life, and driven through storms, but I had never experienced anything like that!

"You're already trying to kill me," Oscar looked over and grinned. "I just got here."

I laughed. "Thank goodness you prayed!"

We pulled into Cheyenne safely and I welcomed Oscar to cowboy town. The next morning, he awoke on the floor, sandwiched atop a deflated air mattress.

"I didn't know it had a hole," I confessed. "But it came with patches!" So much for first impressions, I thought.

We loaded our suitcases into the car to head to Nebraska. Oscar said a prayer before we even left my apartment. I thought I must've really jolted him, because he prayed a lot for safety. It wasn't snowing anymore, but the ground was covered in a thick blanket. We stopped at my usual gas station and bought French vanilla cappuccinos for the road. We'd just begun driving again when Oscar fumbled his, and the whole cup slopped over his lap and onto the floor. The. Entire. Thirty-six. Ounces.

"I'm sorry. I'm sorry," he kept repeating.

"Don't worry. I do that all the time," I shrugged it away. And, I did. Half the time my car smelled of rotten milk. I stopped at the next gas station so he could buy another. One cannot drive a full five hours without a warm cup of coffee, especially on a snowy day.

We got to the Cozad exit roughly four hours later. We still had another hour and fifteen minute drive to Doniphan, but this was the perfect place to fill up on gas and grab some lunch. Plus, Oscar could have a quick look at my hometown before we visited there in a couple of days. We ordered Mexican food at El Paraiso, my favorite Mexican restaurant. It's not really fast food, but we could eat it on the road as we drove. I wanted Oscar to experience Mexican food and this was the best. We pulled back onto the interstate towards Doniphan. We'd driven about ten minutes when I heard, "oh, no!" I looked over. Oscar had dropped enchilada down his chin and down his white-and-blue striped shirt, leaving a big reddish-orange blob in the middle of his chest. "I can't meet your parents like this," he groaned.

I took the Lexington exit and pulled into another gas station. Oscar ruffled through his suitcase, pulled out another shirt, and went inside to change. He sure was spilling a lot! I'd been called clumsy my whole life, but I was starting to believe Oscar might be even clumsier than I was! I didn't get worked up over his spills, though, because I could relate. Oscar got back into the car with his clean shirt on. He was starting to get nervous about meeting my parents now. He was talking more quickly and kept saying, "What if Jim tries to shoot me, Holly? What if he says he's decided he doesn't want a black man in his house?" Oscar knew Jim taught concealed-carry and shooting classes and was very active in the local gun club. This made him incredibly nervous. He'd seen the movies where the father walks out to meet the daughter's date, while cleaning his gun, and he was nervous that Jim might do this.

"Osc, he won't!" I replied. "I promise that, as soon as he meets you, he will love you. He's just leery of you, because he hasn't met you yet." I knew Jim would like Oscar after he met him, because Jim loves respectful, polite young men. Oscar was incredibly polite and had impeccable manners. He always said *please* and *thank you, sir* and *ma'am*. He ate pizza with a knife and fork. He knew the difference between a salad fork and a fish fork, a soup spoon and a dessert spoon. We pulled into the driveway outside of my parent's house. Oscar took a deep breath.

"Hi Tammy, how are you?" Oscar was almost tackled by Mom's embrace. "Hi sir, how are you?" his hand extended into Jim's. They had seen a couple of pictures of Oscar, but I wondered if they still half-thought I'd arrive on their doorstep with a man in a loin cloth with spear in hand. They were surprised: pleasantly surprised. "He's a bit of a pretty boy," Jim whispered my way when Oscar was out of ear shot; "very polite." I grinned to myself.

Over the course of the next few days, Oscar met more and more of my family. Everyone was so nice and welcoming to him. Things seemed to be going well. On Christmas morning, Mom, Bailey, and I worked the morning away getting everything ready. People would be arriving any minute. I went upstairs to check on Oscar. He was sitting on the bed in the spare bedroom. I bent down to give him a hug when my hands met a sticky substance on his lower back. "Oscar, stand up for a minute," I suggested.

"What is it?" Oscar wondered. There on the bed, underneath where Oscar was sitting, lay a now empty tube of Colgate toothpaste. He turned to show me his backside. The bottom of his shirt and the bottom of his pants were covered in toothpaste. The tube had been, once again, full. This time I couldn't hold it in: I laughed hysterically. He was clumsier than I was, that was for sure! I knew he needed to get changed and downstairs quickly, before the rest of the family arrived, but I couldn't stop laughing. I went downstairs and got Mom because the toothpaste was also all over the bedspread. She came upstairs and began laughing hysterically. Oscar laughed an embarrassed laugh. We threw his clothes and the comforter into the washing machine and he changed before anyone arrived.

Things were not going so well for poor Oscar. Spinning on ice. Flat air mattress. Spilled cappuccino. Spilled enchilada. Sat on a tube of toothpaste. The list was growing.

My step-brothers and their families arrived and we all sat down to eat a Christmas lunch of prime rib, shrimp, twice-baked potatoes, and so much more. Mom always makes prime rib for Christmas. Oscar said we Americans eat a lot. In South Africa, it's summer during Christmas, so the meal is similar to what we Americans eat on the Fourth of July. They cook a chicken, ham, or gammon, but they have a lot of cold salads and not many hot dishes or hot drinks. Oscar was enjoying the hot spiced apple cider. We cleared the tables and then all sat around in the living room to open presents. Jim handed all of his sons their presents. That year, two of the boys got .380 semi-automatic pistols.

Oscar whispered into my ear, "Guns. For Christmas?" And then he chuckled in disbelief.

When they started passing them around, I thought Oscar was going to pass out. Oscar had never fired a gun before. In South

Africa, one just doesn't get guns for Christmas, or pass them around to look at. He wondered if this was a Nebraska thing or an American thing. "They could shoot me and bury me out there in the field of snow and no one would find me," he whispered to me; he was serious. My step-brothers encouraged him to hold one, to have a look at it: "the safety is on," they joked. I didn't tell Oscar there were no bullets in the chamber. He took it in his hands for a few seconds, then passed it back. "Guns. For Christmas?" he shook his head at me again and then chuckled a second time.

The Christmas holiday was wonderful. We ice skated on the frozen pond in my parent's backyard; not in ice skates, but in our shoes—gliding around like we were the main characters in a fairytale. It was a winter fairytale, and Oscar taught me how to say just that, in Xhosa. *Itsomi yo busikha* (i-toe-me yo boo-seek-a)—a winter fairytale. Having Oscar in the States was wonderful. We went on dates, went out to coffee, went to church together, prayed together in person, talked about God, and watched DVDs. When the day came to take him back to the airport, I thought my heart would stop beating.

I wore my glasses that day, because I knew I'd cry too much and I didn't want to risk losing a contact: driving back to Wyoming without a contact could have been even more troublesome than the escapade before! I shuffled my feet as slowly as I possibly could as we inched closer and closer to the airport security, and Oscar inched closer and closer to being gone. Tears streamed down my cheeks and my heart felt like a heavy weight inside my chest. Oscar's eyes were watery, "I will see you soon, my queen. Don't cry." I watched him walk through security until I could no longer see him. When I got to my car in the parking lot, I sat in the driver's side seat and sobbed.

CHAPTER TEN

Waka, Waka:
This Time for Africa

I FROZE.

Wyoming iced over in January and I felt myself icing over with it. I was sad and I was lonelier than before. I felt that seeing Oscar had made it worse, because now I knew what I was missing. Spending all that time with my family over the holidays made it all the more apparent that I was now alone again. I read my Bible, read books, continued with work. I let God know I was ready to leave this desert any time now. Oscar had met my family, everything was fine, and I was whole—it was time to go! January turned to February, February turned to March, March turned to April. It was still snowing in Wyoming. The blizzards were so bad a couple of times that I couldn't make it out of my garage in the morning, so I worked from home. The pilot light on my furnace went out three different times, and I could never get the thing to light on my own; I'd come home to a house I could see my breath in.

I enrolled in a belly dance class because I thought it would give me something else to do in the evenings. I was supposed to be studying for my CPA exam, and I did, but I couldn't do that all the time. I thought it might be good for me to belly dance on my honeymoon.

I was a bit nervous that I might have to show my belly, which was no washboard. But I didn't have to . . . at least not until level two, in which you had to do a program and wear a belly dancing outfit. I was certain I would have to repeat level one and then I'd be done, and that would surely be almost like making it to level two. Most of the ladies were in their thirties and forties and most didn't really have washboard stomachs either, so it ended up being okay. I giggled a lot and I think my instructor thought I wasn't taking it seriously. She was hardcore; she wore flowing skirts and went barefoot. I went barefoot too, but I wore sweat pants. Truth be told, I wasn't very good, so I couldn't help but laugh when my belly roll failed to roll and my thighs were still slowing to a jiggle even after I'd stopped shimmying. I almost ordered a shimmy belt, like the other ladies, but they'd been in the class longer, so I thought I would wait until I repeated level one. I watched YouTube videos on belly dancing when I was at home and practiced in the mirror. The instructor said this was the only way to improve. She even said to try to do the belly rolls while we were driving as it was sometimes easier to do a reverse roll. I tried that a couple of times, but I decided I better stick to practicing in the mirror! I could almost do the reverse roll and I could shimmy, though not for long because I got too tired. I couldn't move and shimmy at the same time, that was just way too complicated. So, mostly I could stand and shake like a washing machine on spin cycle, while twirling my hands. I ended up becoming a repeating-level-one-one dropout.

I also helped out with the youth group on Wednesday evenings at the church. I started taking a cycling class at the gym, tried to work-out more, and I joined a women's Bible study on the book of Esther. God was allowing me to experiment, to discover what it was I liked and didn't like, what I enjoyed and didn't enjoy.

I also discovered I liked going for walks and praying. Sometimes I'd walk along the walking trail and watch all of the people. I'd stare at their backs with this deep revelation that I was staring at one of God's children. I wondered if they knew they were His children. I would pray for them while I walked. There were lots of elderly people who walked that trail, some not very fast, so sometimes I'd pray for strength for their legs and feet as I stretched pass them.

Oscar and I had decided that I would come to South Africa in June for the 2010 FIFA World Cup and meet his family. I didn't have a lot of money for my plane ticket, because though I was working, I was paying off a lot of my student debt. I decided I would also start donating plasma to save money. That was something my brother Danny did when he was low on cash, so I thought I could do it too. I would make $20 the first time and $25 the second time, if I gave two times consecutively each week. Plus, I'd read up on how plasma can help save lives, so I thought it was a win-win. I could put it all in savings and save an extra $180 a month.

"I'm literally giving my life's blood to come see you," I told Oscar.

"Holly, are you sure you want to do this," he asked, leery of the situation.

"Absolutely!"

The first time I did it, I did great! I brought a book with me and managed to get forty-five minutes of reading time in. Plus, I read this great story about a little boy who was doing so much better from plasma transfusions. I could still change the world—with my blood. The second time I gave plasma, I nearly vomited and passed out. I decided that I would really have to eat better and drink lots more water on days I donated. I felt sick nearly every second time. My veins were hard to find, so they'd prick one arm, give up, prick the next, go back to the other arm, and then finally get the needle in. That also made me gag. I don't know why, but I couldn't handle the feeling of needles moving and searching underneath my skin. I only donated twice a week for about a month. I was getting sick more and more after about twenty minutes in, so I thought I'd have to find a better way to save money and change the world. I decided I could stop at Starbucks less, even though I'd tried that before.

I was supposed to leave for Johannesburg in the middle of June. The second week in May, I still didn't have enough money saved up to buy my ticket.

"I've prayed about this, Holly, and I'm going to buy your ticket," Oscar stated one evening on Skype.

"Oscar, don't worry, I can still come up with it . . . somehow," I said. "I'm just struggling to come up with the full amount. It's super-expensive with the World Cup going on; tickets are double the normal price. But there's still time, and I will still find a way."

"No, Holly. We need to buy it now. Don't worry, I have the money. You can buy your local flights."

I stepped into the large, circular, arrivals area in the Johannesburg airport, for the first time since I'd arrived in 2009 to volunteer at the orphanage. I felt at home. Within moments, I spotted Oscar, and was soon nestled in his arms.

We arrived late to Oscar's Gran's house. Oscar called his father's employer "Gran." His dad had been working for her for some twenty-odd years and now, in her late eighties, she was like Oscar's grandmother. I was introduced to both Oscar's dad and Gran, and then shown to the guest bedroom, where I would be staying. Once I'd gotten my bags settled in, Oscar and I went out to the garden. He led me beneath a garden archway, which was braided with hot pink roses, and onto the grass. Oscar held me in his arms and we danced there, underneath the stars, spotlighted by the moon.

"One day, we will have this every day," Oscar looked down at me.

"I can't wait," I said, looking up into his eyes. "One day . . ." My voice trailed off.

Gran didn't live far from the church I'd attended when I first came to Johannesburg: the church Oscar still attended. The next morning, we walked through the tree-lined streets to church. Oscar had his arm around me and we were laughing, when we passed two African mamas in their ankle length skirts and head wraps. They looked at us and began clapping, "*Hlala* new South Africa," they cheered. Oscar said something in Zulu.

"What did they say, Osc?"

"Praise the New South Africa," he replied. "They are happy to see black and white joined. 'The New South Africa' is what we call South Africa after apartheid. They are happy to see a true picture of it." I smiled to myself; hlala New South Africa, hlala Lord!

After church, Oscar's Dad dropped us off at the train station. We were taking it to the airport to catch our flight to Durban for the Germany versus Australia soccer match. I don't remember much about the game. It was a night game. I sat in those stands at the Moses Mabhida Stadium, high above the field, looking across the stadium and up into the sky. I didn't want any of it to end. I looked over at Oscar with the German flag painted on his cheek, and I felt his excitement. My heart swelled. I loved this man. I loved that we shared the same interests and values; that we thoroughly enjoyed one another's company and conversation. As I looked up at the sky, I knew I could choose; and I wanted to choose a life married to this man, living in this very country, surrounded by these very people. We caught a red-eye flight back to Johannesburg that night and arrived around 4 a.m. I was tired, but I didn't mind. The adventure was worth it. Who needed sleep? We would lengthen the short span of time we had together and we would make the best of it.

We were up early the next morning. We had tickets to watch Denmark play the Netherlands at the Soccer City Stadium near

Soweto, outside of Johannesburg. I hadn't known that Oscar liked soccer so much. He'd told me he had purchased tickets and I knew he liked soccer, but obviously I had underestimated how much.

Energy and excitement pulsed through the crowd, and people from all over the world danced and cheered to the beat of vuvuzelas. The atmosphere was electric! Shakira's song "Waka, Waka" came over the loudspeakers. I stood next to Oscar, who was dipping his hips and bobbing his shoulders to the beat, bumping into me. He wore a permanent smile. I watched the woman in front of me shake her hips like I'd never seen before. I watched her four-year-old do the same and my jaw dropped. After a few moments of observing, I thought I had the technique down. I tried it. I don't know what I looked like, but I felt like a bobber at the end of a fishing line, bouncing up and down across the water. Straight up, straight down as I tried to catch the beat. I stopped.

"You dance like a white girl," Oscar laughed.

"Well, what else did you expect," I grinned back.

A day later, while South Korea's team warmed up, the Argentina team kicked soccer balls into the net on the opposite side of the field. Amanda sat next to me. Kali sat next to Oscar. The four of us hadn't been together since that night in 2009 when we stood outside Mugg & Bean. We were at our third soccer match of the World Cup in just four days. Shakira's song came over the loud speaker again. One line in the song says, "People are raising their expectations. Today's the day." I looked around the stadium at all the people. This was a soccer match, but I saw more. I was raising my expectations. I wanted more. I wanted to live an adventure, always, no matter where I was. I wanted to choose the life God had for me, the plans He had for me, even if they didn't make sense—to me or to the rest of the world. I wanted to raise my expectations and I wanted to keep raising them. My Father is the King of the Universe, the Author and Creator of the world, so I thought I could expect a lot more than what I'd previously been accepting. It wasn't just about jet-setting across the continent or going to World Cup matches. It wasn't about some romantic love story. It was about raising my expectations to believe that God had a life for me, in the spiritual and in the physical, so much more wonderful than I could even begin to comprehend. He could draw me closer to Himself and He could draw me closer to His exceedingly abundant plan for my life. Yes, I was raising my expectations!

> Now unto Him that is able to do exceedingly abundantly above all we ask or think, according to the power that worketh in us.
>
> – Ephesians 3:20 (KJV)

I was nervous. I was going to meet Oscar's mom. I knew she had a hard time accepting the fact that Oscar was dating a white woman. When he first told her, her response was, "Are you trying to kill me?" At least if he didn't seriously date a Xhosa woman, he could have at least dated another black girl, she thought. I didn't want somebody to wish I was black, just like a black person wouldn't want someone to wish they were white. But I would love her son just the same. I couldn't imagine how difficult it must be for her to have her son bring me home. And not just a white woman, but an *American* woman. She feared I would take her son away—that I'd fly him off to my country and she'd never see him again. She was just like my mom: she didn't want her baby taken away, so far away, from her. I had talked to his mom on Skype a couple of times and she was very kind and sweet, but I knew it wasn't easy for her. I knew she wondered how this was going to work out, how I would interact with the rest of the family. I didn't blame her. This wasn't what she'd imagined, and I wasn't who she imagined her son would bring home.

Oscar's mom came into the room and hugged me. She reached out her hands and draped a dark green and brown satin scarf around my neck. I watched her slender, dark fingers tie it. "Welcome to our family," she smiled. I wrapped my arms around her again. The scarf was her favorite scarf and she gave it to me as a symbol of her welcoming me into the family. This wasn't an ideal situation for her, but she would accept it, she would welcome it. I couldn't speak Xhosa and she preferred to speak her language, as opposed to English. She often spoke to Oscar in Xhosa and then Oscar would fill me in on the details later. I didn't know her traditions; I didn't know the expectations of a woman in Xhosa culture. She had a home, had family, in a village where there was no indoor plumbing or indoor water. An outhouse sat out back of her house. Rainwater was collected in what they often called a jojo tank: a tank used to harvest the water for use. *If* Oscar married me, I would need to go to her home, meet her family. But I was from America. I would be different. I might make them uncomfortable. (Little did she know that I had had my own experiences with no indoor plumbing in India, and I was now a pro!) Regardless, she made a choice. And, she tied that choice firmly around my neck.

All too soon, my week of vacation was over. It was time to fly back to Wyoming, and my heart poured down my face.

"I don't want to go," I clung to Oscar. "I don't want to leave here, I don't want to leave you."

"I don't want you to, either," Oscar squeezed me tighter.

"It's worse getting left," he said. "When I left you it was hard, but this is worse: being left behind. It won't be for long, Rene." Oscar had also started calling me by my middle name as a nickname. I went with that too.

I shuffled my feet as slowly as possible through the security line, looking back at Oscar every few seconds. He stood there waiting, just as I had, until I was out of sight. The further I inched along, the further I inched to his last glance and last wave. There would be no turning back. I wanted to run back. I wanted to drop my backpack, miss my plane, and stay in South Africa. *Why, Lord, am I still in Wyoming? Why do I have to go back to being an auditor? When am I going to marry this man and move?*

The lady next to me on the flight kept stealing side glances. I couldn't help my blubbering and sniffling. The more I tried to shush myself, the more my chest heaved. She didn't say a word. I cried myself to sleep and when I woke up a few hours later, I cried again. When my final flight landed in Denver, I thought I'd descended into the underworld. I stomped my feet across the parking lot in long-term parking, wheeling my suitcase in a fury as I got back into my car and back onto I–25 north to Cheyenne. I called Mom on the drive home, blubbered to her about how miserable I was and how I was ready for God to get me out of the desert. She reassured me that in His time, He would make a way. She asked me if I wanted to move back home. I told her yes. She said she'd talk to Jim.

I wheeled my suitcase into my empty apartment and plopped it onto the ground. I wasn't going to unpack. I wasn't going to do a thing. I crawled into bed and skyped Oscar, then I fell asleep. I was so tired I slept most of the next day. I cried to God. *This is so hard. How am I supposed to be content in all things when I don't like anything around me?*

That's not true, He whispered. I was reminded that I actually liked a lot of things around me. I was just throwing my toys around. Still!

It was towards the end of June when I got back from Johannesburg. The following week, I asked a lady in our church if she'd mentor me.

She said yes. We met for coffee and started going through a book together. She invited me to her house and taught me how to make sourdough starter and homemade bread. I joined one of the Bible studies she was in and we started to go through Beth Moore's book *So Long Insecurity*. I realized I was really insecure. The deeper I got into the book, the more insecurities I realized I had. I decided to pray for more God-given confidence. I was starting to enjoy myself in Cheyenne. I went to the gym a lot, would make dinner for myself on a Friday night, then curl up and read a book. On Saturdays, after I'd skyped with Oscar, when I should have been studying for my CPA, I'd go to Starbucks and study a little, then rent a DVD, or write. I watched a lot of DVDs. Sometimes I took myself to the movie. Sometimes, I'd have dinner with a couple of friends from work. I'd never had so few friends in a place I'd lived. God became my best friend. I'm not just speaking "Christian-ese" here; He really did. I talked to Him like He was my roommate. Sometimes I told Him He had to come up with His share of the rent, and He miraculously would.

One afternoon, after I'd finished a grocery trip to Wal-Mart and was loading groceries into the trunk of my car, I looked across the parking lot and saw a whole flock of birds eating behind a parked car. That's one sure way to get run over, I thought. But then I looked a little closer at what they were frantically pecking away at; it was a spilled box of Lucky Charms, marshmallows and all.

God, you really do provide for the birds of the air, just like you say, I told him. *And that isn't some lousy bird food, that's dessert!* I got stuck on that picture for a while. I sat thinking about those birds eating Lucky Charms. God provides for His creation; just sometimes not how His creation expects. I felt as if God asked me, just as He does in that verse in Matthew 6, *are you not more valuable than they?* And, I am more valuable. You're more valuable. God said so himself, so why do I question it? Why do I worry about God's provision when I can see His provision everywhere? Sometimes I just need to stop for a moment and see the provision; see what the birds are doing; see the Lucky Charms spilled all over the parking lot. I came to know God as a God not only who provides, but who provides dessert. And dessert in the desert! How much better is that!? Once again, it's exceedingly and abundantly more than we need or ask for.

Oscar had been bringing up marriage more and more. He asked me lots of hypothetical questions. Like, hypothetically, if he did propose, would I want to move to South Africa? He wondered if, when it came down to it, would I truly want to leave the United States? I told him I absolutely would! I loved South Africa and I missed it. I'd heard a sermon in which the preacher said he felt like he had been born in the United States, but made in South Africa. I decided that's how I felt. I was born in the United States and I loved it, but I felt made in South Africa, as if that's where God started to really put me together.

Nearly every morning, I'd put on a pot of coffee and sit on the floor in my living room right beside my patio doors and read the Bible. I don't say nearly every morning because I made a pot of coffee nearly every morning. I made that every day. I say nearly every morning, because reading my Bible happened more *nearly* than *every*. I'd stare out at the trees, at the street, and pray. I prayed for a lot of things, but mostly I prayed that God would help me praise Him where I was, help me be content where I was, and help me to wait patiently on Him. I felt like we were encircled in a continuous sweet moment with just each other. A sweet time—just God and me.

My mentor and I were meeting regularly. Another church was putting on a women's teaching event that would meet every week for a couple of months. We would worship, have a message, and then break up in small groups to go through the Bible study that paralleled the message. Women from any church were welcome. I volunteered to facilitate a group, only to realize that I, at twenty-four, was facilitating a group of women between thirty-five and fifty. There were girls my age who attended the church, but this was the small group assigned to me. I was terrified.

I felt inadequate, under-qualified, and insecure; not ready! (I know. Even after reading the book.) Then God reminded me of a scripture in First Timothy. It says, "Do not let anyone look down on you because you are young, but be an example for believers in speech, in conduct, in love, in faith and in purity" (I Timothy 4:12). I decided I would try to be an example, even in my youth. My voice shook when I asked questions. The women were so kind, so wonderful, and after a couple of weeks I was fine. I still had to travel out of town a lot, so when I had to be away during the week, another woman would fill in for me.

The church was located on a hill just outside of town. I remember driving home one evening and thinking of the verse in Second Chronicles where it says the eyes of the Lord range throughout the earth to strengthen those whose hearts are fully committed to Him. I looked across the rugged hills in the night sky and at the desolate prairie grass. Wyoming was such a vast place. I thought it funny that of all the places on the earth, the Lord's eyes had ranged to this place and strengthened me. I was grateful to Him for finding me. I was grateful to Him for searching me out, for ranging his eyes to and fro across the earth for me, for promising to strengthen me. If your heart is committed to Him, I'm certain His eyes are ranging across the earth to strengthen you too. That's who God is and what He's about—He finds us exactly where we are.

One Sunday afternoon, I was driving back to Wyoming from a visit to Nebraska, and praying to God. I felt like my time in Wyoming was nearing an end. You know, like when you feel the wind shifting and in a subtle, knowing way, you're aware that the season is changing. I wasn't stomping my feet anymore, and I asked God if I could, pretty please, move. I still didn't like being an auditor, and I knew that as soon as I left Wyoming, I'd never do it again. I loved spreadsheets and financial statements, but the job bored me completely. I prayed every day on the way to work that I'd make it through the day and be able to give it my all; and I did . . . mostly.

It was August. Oscar would be coming back to the States in December again, and I was almost certain he was going to propose. I was also almost certain that when we married I would move to South Africa, but I wanted to be closer to my family. Driving five hours to and from Nebraska was a lot of driving for a weekend, and I knew with work I would be lucky to visit one weekend a month. I was reminded of a seasonal tax company that hired a number of temporary workers before tax season. I decided I would contact the company's office in a town just twenty minutes away from Mom's house. It was time.

When I got back to my apartment in Wyoming, I sat down at my computer and researched the company in Nebraska. I took the online tax exam to test my knowledge, and had my score emailed to the owner of the company. A couple of days later, I received a phone call and was told to come in when I got back to Nebraska. I wasn't sure I would get this job, but I was certain there was a pretty good chance, because they would have to quadruple the staff in order to make it through tax season.

Jim said I could move back home. I didn't really know how long it would be or what would happen, but I decided I would move anyway. In October, I wrote my resignation letter and turned it in. Thirty days later, two days before Thanksgiving, I headed back to Nebraska.

I was sad to say goodbye to my mentor at church. I felt like I'd finally settled into my life in the desert in the four months prior to leaving, and it was hard to believe it was now over. I didn't fully know what lay ahead. I looked back at the rugged hills through my rearview mirror as I drove back east and to Nebraska. I would no longer be "forever west," forever! I had cried when I first entered Wyoming, I had irrigated that desert the entire time I was there, and as I drove away, tears pooled in the corners of my eyes once more.

CHAPTER ELEVEN

The Diamond

I BONDED.

I had always thought that I'd feel like a loser if, at the age of twenty-four, I moved back home with my parents. I didn't. It was fantastic! Bailey, though, who was fourteen at the time and accustomed to living as an only child, didn't find it fantastic. She started calling me "Dr. Phil," which I actually took as a compliment, though she didn't mean it that way. I frequently heard, "Shut up, Dr. Phil. Moooommmmm, tell her to stop it." Of course, Mom told her not to say "shut up." Mom also suggested I keep my lessons and philosophies to myself because Bailey was only fourteen, and well, she just didn't understand.

So, I busied myself preparing for Oscar's arrival and for Christmas. I booked a suite at the Mountain View Hotel, a bed-and-breakfast in Centennial, Wyoming. A historic hotel nestled at the foot of the Snowy Range Mountains, I thought this would be the perfect, quaint place to spend a couple of days before Christmas. It had a separate living room with a sleeper couch and a bedroom with two queen beds. It could sleep six comfortably. There would be only the two of us, which is why we needed it to have a separate living room and why we needed it to sleep as many as possible. The more space, the better. We were, after all, crazy about each other but waiting until marriage to consummate our relationship. I planned to take Oscar skiing, which he had never done before. His birthday was also in December, so as a surprise, I booked a half day of snowmobiling in the mountains.

Less than a month later, I picked Oscar up at the airport. We drove slowly into the town of Centennial, the snow falling and piling around us. We arrived late for our snowmobile booking; driving an Oldsmobile Alero up into the mountains, during winter, wasn't the smartest thing I'd ever decided to do. I didn't have a pickup or 4x4, but I was willing to do whatever it took for Oscar to have this new adventure.

We finally pulled up at a log cabin, the office of Snowy Range Tours in the Snowy Range Mountains. Oscar was already freezing, so we quickly changed into the snow boots, helmets, and snow gloves provided. Then Oscar and I, along with the tour guide, saddled our snowmobiles. After a few brief instructions, we were on our way, zipping across a white ocean of snow. I marveled at the pine trees whose tops barely peaked above the layers of packed snow, the powder flying away to my right and left. It was as if we were in Narnia, the iced-over Narnia of the White Witch's rule. I was lost in that fairytale, that magical wonder of God's beauty and glory, when Oscar beached his snowmobile and tipped off. The instructor got off of his snowmobile, unburied Oscar's, and drove it out. We pressed the throttles again and shot back out over the snow. I leaned forward, lifted myself off of the seat, and flew faster, swerving to the right, to the left. The wind beat against my helmet. Surrounded by white feathered pine trees and mountains of snow, it felt as if we were only a mile from Heaven. Oscar beached his snowmobile again and tipped off.

"This is a blast!" Oscar exclaimed. "But I'm really cold. How long is this going to last?"

"I booked a half-day," I exulted, "and we've only been riding for thirty minutes. We still have almost four hours left."

"Hols, I don't think I can do four hours. It's so cold. And the altitude is so high that I'm struggling to breathe. You forget I'm from Africa."

So we decided to ride just a short while more. The instructor once again dug Oscar's snowmobile out and drove it back onto the packed snow, and we once again pressed our throttles. Oscar sped off in front of me, looking back to make sure I was watching. He leaned forward, swerved to the left, swerved to the right, then looked back at me again. I could picture his smile through his helmet, almost hear him revving along with the engine. He tailed the instructor, held his throttle down further . . . and then he beached it again.

By this time, I could tell the instructor was getting irritated and tired of having to dig Oscar's snowmobile out of the snow. We rode for an hour and a half before Oscar could no longer brave the cold.

"This was the best birthday present I've ever gotten, Hols."

"I'm so glad, Oscar. I wanted to give you an adventure."

"This was the best adventure; you are my biggest adventure," he hugged me through our puffy coats.

The recent snowfall blocked the entryway and parking lot in front of the historic hotel, so we parked on the side of the road and trekked inside. Our suite was rustic and homey. The sleeper couch was a striped dark green, maroon, and light brown. The headboards of the two queen beds were carved out of wood and were painted the color of wheat. Matching white quilts, detailed with green and maroon triangle and diamond shapes, covered the beds. We would spend the next two days skiing, so we went to sleep early.

Around four a.m. the next morning, I heard Oscar rustling around in the living room. I opened my eyes to see light streaming through the bottom of the closed door. I fell back asleep.

"Hols, Hols, please wake up," Oscar shook me with a hushed whisper.

"Please wake up. I haven't been able to sleep."

"What time is it?" I asked.

"Just after five. Please, will you turn on the light, read the note on your bedside stand, and then come out into the living room?"

I got up, turned on the light, and read the note he'd placed on my nightstand. Half-awake, I walked into the living room. The song "Malibongwe" was playing from the laptop. This was one of the worship songs we sang when I first visited South Africa in 2009. It was my favorite. And I recognized the voice singing. It was one of my friends who sang in the worship band at church. Oscar had had her record it for me. The words softly echoed into the early-morning stillness.

Ngaphandle kwakho, anginathemba, anginalutho
(Without you I have no hope, I have nothing)
Ngaphandle kwakho, Ngaphandle kwakho
(Without you, without you)
Wangifela esiphambanweni, Wangikhipha ezonweni zam
(You died for me at the cross, You cleansed me of my sins)
Ngasho ngahlala nawe iNkosi, Ngasho ngahlala nawe iNkosi
(And I get to dwell with you God, And I get to dwell with you God)
Malibongwe igama lakho, Malibongwe igama lakho)
(Let your name be praised, Let your name be praised)

Malibongwe igama, Malibongwe igama,
(Let your name, let your name)
Malibongwe igama lakho
(Let your name be praised)
Malibongwe, Malibongwe
(Be praised, be praised)

Malibongwe, Malibongwe
(Be praised, be praised)

Oscar reached his hands towards my cheeks; they were trembling. He began to pray. I closed my eyes, cheeks jiggling because his hands were shaking so much. Oscar dropped to his knee with the ring box in hand and said: "Holly Rene Kostman, will you do me the honor of becoming my wife?" his voice cracked.

I looked down at him and into his eyes, "Yes! I will!"

"Did you say yes?" Oscar asked.

"Yes! I said, yes!"

"I thought you might jump up and down and scream or something," Oscar replied.

"Well, it is 5 a.m. And, I haven't had my coffee yet."

"I'm sorry, I just couldn't wait. I thought of a million ways to do this. And I had a plan in my head, but I couldn't sleep last night and I just couldn't wait any longer. I had to ask you. Now!"

"It's okay! I love it now! We can't phone anyone or let them know yet, it's too early, so we can share this moment for the next two hours: just the two of us!"

"I had thought I might ask you while we were at the top of the mountain, before we skied down. But it was too much! The surprise was too much to hold in!"

"It's okay, Osc! I loved this! It was perfect! You proposed to worship music, after a prayer, and what could be more perfect than proposing with God right at the center?"

Oscar and I waited a few hours and then relayed the news to family and friends. Then we headed off to the ski slopes.

It's a good thing Oscar didn't wait to propose at the top of the mountain, because it would have been at the top of the bunny slope, with the kiddies. He spent the entire day falling down the bunny slope.

"Osc, now put your skis together like a pizza slice, and try to control your knees and ankles as you're trying to stop."

"Pizza slice, pizza slice, pizzzzzaaaa sliiiiicccee!" Oscar yelled down the bunny slope as he fell to a stop halfway down. By his fifth attempt, his pants were soaked through and snow had burrowed into his boots. He couldn't get to the bottom of the slope without falling. Kids skied past him and he shook his head in disbelief: "I don't like skiing!" he exclaimed.

His skis got criss-crossed on the ski escalator more than once, causing a bottle neck and a backed-up line of kids more than willing to try to assist.

"You can do it, Osc! You just have to get used to it. Believe in yourself!" I encouraged him.

Oscar finally made it to a point where he could make it to the bottom of the bunny slope before falling to a stop. However, this method of stopping himself occurred right in the pathway of the rest of the learners, who then had to try to avoid crashing into him—at times without success! I couldn't help but laugh. I laughed so hard and for so long that he began to take offense. This was not how my tough, athletic rugby player had imagined the day would go! Always good at sports, he had assumed he'd cruise down the slopes with style and ease. Having to have little kids help him was embarrassing.

With only an hour left before the resort closed for the day, I convinced Oscar to move from the bunny slope to the green, beginner trail. The ski lift operator stopped the ski lift altogether so he could climb on board. I prepped Oscar the whole way to the top on how to get out of the ski chair and off of the lift. Despite my instructions, we both ended in a tangled heap at the base of the exit slope.

"It could've been worse, Osc! Don't worry, we got up quickly!"

By the end of the second day, Oscar could get on the ski chair without the operator stopping or slowing it. So he had made progress. But he decided that skiing was exhausting and challenging, and he hadn't decided if he actually enjoyed it.

The following day, while the stars still pierced bits of early morning darkness, we drove the icy roads back to Nebraska at a cautious pace. We celebrated our engagement, Christmas, and New Years with my family, and set the date for our wedding for the 23rd of July. Before I knew it, it was time for Oscar to fly back to Johannesburg. My heart still melted visibly down my cheeks as I hugged him goodbye at the airport. It would only be goodbye for four months, but it was difficult, nevertheless. Goodbye was and is always hard for me, whether it's a short goodbye or a long goodbye. Watching someone walk away while you have to remain is never easy.

I stayed behind in Nebraska, living with my parents, soaking up time with family, working to save money, and planning the wedding. Bailey frequently told me she was going to buy my plane ticket back to South Africa—right then! I told her that would be great, because they were expensive. I thought that God had changed my heart so much that I'd take my little sister for manicures and we would watch movies together and do Bible studies about being a young woman. But we mostly fought.

My sister is ten years younger than me, but she is taller, stronger, and scarier. I still run from her. When she was in middle school, around the time she shaved half her eye brow off, a girl in her class called her fat. Bailey knocked her down on the playground, then sat on top of her, and shoved her face into the gravel. She's the type of girl who sent a shiver down my spine in school. My sister.

I was disappointed with myself, because I had moved back home wanting to improve relationships and bond with my family before I moved to South Africa. I didn't realize that relationship was so hard. In Wyoming, I was mostly alone, so I didn't really have to relate to anyone; I did what I wanted to do, and I only had to listen to myself. I didn't realize that though God had done a work on my heart in Wyoming, He still had a lot more work to do. After all, it's easy to be nice and get along with yourself and be a good person when no one is around to irritate you!

I also moved back home with great intentions of serving; I was going to serve my entire family. I would clean for Mom and help around the house, and anticipate their needs and get them drinks or snacks while they were watching TV. One afternoon when Mom was in the kitchen and I was lying on the couch watching TV, I yelled up to her, "Mom, will you bring me a glass of water and an orange?" When I heard myself, the expectation in my tone, it dawned on me: I was a terrible servant. Why was it so easy to *plan* how great a sister or daughter or friend I was going to be, and then so difficult to actually be it? I had the best of intentions, but little success in acting out those intentions.

Mom and I worked out a lot together, trying to get into shape to wear our wedding dresses. We watched *Criminal Minds* every evening while we made flower bouquets and centerpieces. Mom is creative with arts and crafts, and very patient. She's also patient when wrapping presents. When we do it together, I try to find all of the presents that fit into bags and let Mom do the actual wrapping. Mom is like a bubble of joy, filled with an abundance of life. Jim would even go as far as to suggest she's even full of bubbles. Sometimes I'd get too deep for Mom and she'd look at me with a "you-lost-me-five minutes-ago" type of face. She'd then do something like throw her banana peel out the car window and towards the country ditch while saying, "I hope nobody slips!" We'd then laugh hysterically, imagining the cartoons depicting when that actually happened. Mom always said we could throw biodegradable stuff towards the ditch if we were on a country road, as long as it was biodegradable. So we still purposely try to eat bananas in the car, so we can throw it out the window, off a country road, and hope nobody slips.

One afternoon, when mom and I were driving home from picking up my wedding dress, a song came on the Christian radio station we were listening to. I hadn't heard it played in years. Mom and I were silenced as the words filled the car: *"This hand is bitterness, we want to taste it and let the hatred numb our sorrows. The wise hand opens slowly to lilies of the valley and tomorrow; this is what it feels to be held."* It was the song we had played at Dad's funeral. I sat with goose bumps covering my arms and legs. I thought of Dad. On the day I picked up my wedding dress, I felt like my Heavenly Father gave me a gift—the one song that most reminded me of Dad. The song that made me feel close to him, that I associated with him. And on that day, with my wedding dress in the backseat, I knew what it felt like to be held. I had been held all along.

Bailey designed the ring bearer's pillow she was going to sew. Having lived with Dad since I was eleven, so having never grown up with Bailey apart from some summers and weekends, I realized how much I'd missed out on with both her and Mom.

Bailey and I slowly got closer, though she still referred to me as Dr. Phil. I learned that my free advice and input were more appreciated when asked for. If she wanted it, she would come to me for it. And the less I streamed it from a megaphone in her ears, the closer she moved towards me and the more open she became to it. I never served like I wanted to serve and I didn't achieve best friend status with my little sister; mostly, I just realized how incredibly in need of Christ I was. When my high-pitched screams made contact with Bailey's heart, I couldn't believe I actually called myself a Christian.

Christ-ian. "-Ian" is a suffix which is attached to the end of words to indicate a likeness, a resembling, a belonging to, or having a profession in. A historian. A politician. A Romanian. A historian professes history. A politician is a person who belongs to politics. A Romanian is someone belonging to, or resembling, Romania. I could profess being a Christian all I wanted, but the truth was, even after all my Bible readings, all my life lessons, all of my efforts, I didn't resemble Christ. I belonged to Christ, I professed Christ, but I wasn't like Christ; not yet. I realized that I was on this never-ending journey of becoming like Him, and I would become more and more like Him, but it would be a process, not simply a quick prayer.

I had thought I could simply pray a lot of prayers and then I'd walk around loving like Christ and serving like Christ, floating like an ethereal woman on a cloud of peace and kindness. That cloud burst relatively quickly. And it would only continue to evaporate. I would have to learn to be like Christ in the dust and in the grit. Dust caked His sandaled feet from walking the long road, the hard road, on His encounters with hurt, pain, rejection, fear, and other people's hatred of Him. On those dusty roads, those hard roads, He responded with a Heavenly perspective and with a Godly reaction. I would have to choose that perspective and choose those reactions. He would grace me and teach me about love, self-control, and kindness, but I would have to walk those attributes out when it was hardest for me to do so.

While I was back in Nebraska, I spent some time with Grandma Rose. I looked at her old wedding album, asking her questions about her own wedding. One afternoon as I sat drinking coffee in her front living room, I asked Grandma if she thought Dad would have had a problem with the fact that Oscar was black. Some who knew Dad alluded, in no subtle words, to the fact that he wouldn't be happy with my choice. As the wedding was nearing, I thought more and more about this. I thought they might be right. I'd heard some comments Dad had made in passing, in joking, and I wondered.

Grandma said Dad probably would have struggled at first just because it was different and not what he would have expected. She said he would have come over to her house, sat down for a cup of coffee, just like I was having now, and talked. But he would've been okay with it in the end. Dad never hated anyone. Dad hadn't experienced much culture or color different from his own. I determined that, surrounded by what was familiar, Dad based his expectations and dreams for me on what he knew, on what surrounded us at the time. I knew that, deep down, he would want me to be with someone who treated me like gold. If he were still alive, I believed, in time, he wouldn't care about the color of those hands that treated me like gold.

I also tried to spend as much time as possible with Danny, though it wasn't as much time as I wanted. Sometimes I'd go to his house and listen to him play guitar. Other times we'd have TV marathons, and watch as many seasons as we could of a series. Danny and I were even closer than we'd been before. After Dad's death, when he'd been going through a rough patch and needed to get out of my hometown, I moved him down to Kearney to stay with me, before finding him a place to live. One night as we were talking before bed, Danny got very quiet.

"Holly?"

"Yes, Danny?"

"The thing I regret most in life is that I didn't stay with Dad; that day I left." And then Danny's voice got shaky and he started to cry. I started to cry too. In that moment, I wished I could have given him the moment I'd shared with Dad. I wished he could've had it. I wished I could have turned back time. I knew that his statement was only the beginning of the level of pain Danny was feeling. And I knew that the choices he had been making, the lifestyle he'd been living, were all attempts at trying to numb that pain.

During the time that Danny lived with me, he got up nearly every morning at the same time I did and we read our Bibles together. I'd made Danny the Indian tea recipe from India and he was the only one, other than me, who loved it. I made Indian tea every day. And if I didn't make it, Danny asked me to make it. We sat, sipping our tea, and reading our Bibles together. I wanted to give Danny a fresh start, I wanted every action and decision from his past to be wiped clean, and I wanted him to live as who he was created to be. I couldn't give that to Danny, though. There was only One who could. All I could do was tell Danny more and more about Him, and pray that he chose Him and continued to choose Him.

Danny was the hardest person for me to consider leaving when I said yes to move to South Africa. Each time I thought about leaving my brother, I cried. He'd grown up with me, shared one of the world's deepest hurts with me. He was my brother and I didn't know if he was going to be okay. Who would take care of Danny if I left? I knew Mom would, but there's such a different bond between a sister and a brother. Danny could look at me and know my heart in an instant. I could look at his and know it as well. I wanted to protect him; shield him from the world; shield him from the efforts of the Enemy to rob him of the life God had for him. I didn't want any more bad things to happen to Danny and I didn't want him to choose any more bad things.

Danny was my little brother; my little brother who I felt needed me. Who was going to be his protector? I remember once, Mom sent Danny and me to an afterschool day care center. I hated that day care. First, because I was in fifth grade and still had to go to day care when most of my classmates didn't. It was right across the street from my school, so every day the workers from the day care made us line up, in front of everyone, and march across the street to day care. So all my classmates knew that I was still going to day care. I also didn't like it because it was called *Grow, Learn and Play,* but there was no playing that occurred there; at least none that I remember. Nearly every day they put Danny in timeout. I knew Danny wasn't being *that* naughty. He just played hard. One day, I told the caretaker that I was tired of her picking on my brother, that he was just playing, and she always got mad at him. She then sat me in timeout too, and when I responded with, "now you're picking on me!", I ended up sitting there until Mom came to pick us up. As soon as Mom picked us up, I told her everything that happened. Mom knew I never got into trouble, only with her, and she'd been tired of Danny always being in timeout, so she thought we were probably telling the truth: they were picking on Danny—and now picking on me too, I assured her! Not long after that, Mom took us out of day care and got us an in-home babysitter.

God, who will look out for Danny like a big sister? I cried. *I will, Holly. I will. But not like a big sister, like the father he's missing,* He whispered. And God would. I trusted God, but it was one of the hardest things I'd ever done to let go of my brother and trust God to look out for Him. I realized later that I had an unhealthy savior complex. I was never meant to save Danny. I was not my brother's savior. Jesus is.

In May, without any monetary contribution from Bailey, I boarded a plane for South Africa: to volunteer in the orphanage, once again, and to attend pre-marriage counseling with Oscar. We thought it best to do pre-marriage counseling at the church we were going to attend once we were married, the same church we met at in 2009. We would fly back to the States before the wedding, and then fly back to South Africa after the wedding and honeymoon.

CHAPTER TWELVE

Hot Chocolate in June

I UNDERESTIMATED.

I underestimated the amount of grief I would feel over leaving home, leaving my family, leaving the United States. I had been longing for South Africa from the moment the plane lifted off from there in 2009. Now I was about to taste Africa again—but this time it would be permanent. Though I would be returning to the States for our wedding and would be seeing my family again soon, I felt as though I was leaving for good. I hugged Mom at the airport and felt a great loss, that aching loss of a child leaving her mother, leaving home. I was becoming a "big girl" and I was stepping out on my own two feet as a woman, but those steps were taking me very far away. There was an enormity in leaving everything.

We held a garage sale two weeks before I left. I had to sort through my belongings, assigning levels of importance to each item. I'd pick through clothes, decorations, books, furniture, and it would either be coming to South Africa with me, stored at Mom and Jim's, or sold. Unfortunately, there was a limit to what I could store at Mom and Jim's. There was also a limit to what would fit in my suitcases. I sold most all of my furniture, lots of my clothes, my car, and most of my belongings. I kept the things that had sentimental value and a few things I thought I might one day want.

The day I sold my car, a lump formed in my throat and my eyes welled up. Dad had helped me pick out that car two months before he got sick. My previous car had been breaking down a lot and he had to fix it constantly. Dad's life insurance money also paid off the balance of my car loan. So, when I placed the keys of my Oldsmobile Alero into the hands of someone else, I felt like I was handing over the last remnants of Dad. I'd acquired so much over the short years of my life and in all the dreaming, I hadn't thought about the reality of selling nearly all I had. But was all that stuff what really mattered? It was, after all, just stuff.

I brought two over-stuffed suitcases on the first trip, and Oscar and I would each bring two over on our way back. Four and a half suitcases. My life's belongings would be reduced to four and a half suitcases, and some boxes in a closet and in the crawl space at Mom and Jim's house.

I really thought I would be able to easily leave my homeland, with little emotion, because I loved South Africa and Oscar so much. I thought the goodbye would be easy, because I had such a deep longing and anticipation for this new adventure, this new life. But the old and the familiar were difficult to leave. I felt the ache of leaving my family, my friends, and all I had really ever known. I felt the grief of loss.

Starting just a few days after my arrival, Oscar and I began to fight. Each day, the boxing gloves of my words jabbed my fiancé, and I raised fists to my chin to block the returning blows. I fought with Oscar like you wouldn't believe. We were attending pre-marriage counseling and we were learning how to communicate effectively, love effectively, and handle conflict effectively. We didn't do it so effectively.

"Just take this ring!" I yelled. "You can have it back!" I announced as I yanked my ring off my finger and shoved it, in extended hand, towards Oscar. I had vowed I would never do this!

"Holly, I can't believe you would do that. That you would take your ring off and try to give it back to me!" He shook his head in disbelief. He wouldn't take it.

I stayed at the orphanage and volunteered from roughly 6 a.m. to 6 p.m. each weekday. Oscar would pick me up for dinner in the evening and drop me back off at the orphanage a few hours later. We would then spend Saturday and Sunday together, on my days off.

We did not get along. We fought every day and about the most insignificant things. I wondered if this was the cultural difference people talked about. I wondered if it was the result of dating long-distance for nearly two years and not spending a lot of time together. This was the love of my life, and this was no fairytale. It was hard. This was relationship, and it was tough.

"You are a *****!" I screamed—and I don't swear. Oscar had just told me I was acting like a cow. He had done nothing wrong; I really had done nothing wrong, until we started fighting. Then we both did it utterly wrong. My heart was hardening and I didn't know if I *wanted* to love this man, even though he was the best man I'd ever known. His heart was hardening, and he was deciding whether he wanted to choose to love this woman.

"Let's go to the park, have a picnic, and talk. Let's talk, Holly! Calmly!" Oscar pleaded.

"I don't want to have a picnic with you! That's the last thing I want to do, Oscar! I would be faking I would be faking it trying to sit there and eat when I DO NOT WANT TO BE AROUND YOU!" I let him have it.

Oscar packed a blanket and a large pizza in the car and told me to get in. He spread the blanket across the grass at the park and opened up the box of pizza. "Go on, eat," he suggested.

I ate. One slice. Two slices. Three slices. Four slices. I stretched out on my stomach and rested my head on my arms. I looked over at Oscar. I did love this man. He just did things that irritated me and said things in a way I didn't understand. We would then fight because I didn't understand what he was actually saying. When I was driving in the car and he said "indicate right" instead of "turn right" and I put my blinker on but kept driving straight, I didn't know that *indicate* meant *turn*. I just thought it meant turn your blinker on. When I said I was going to miss my family and the efficiencies and options in the United States, I didn't mean that I was miserable and blamed him that I didn't have all my usual comforts: I just meant I would miss them.

I heard a story once about a man who used to go crazy because his wife would not fill up the ice cube tray after each use. He stressed again and again how she should fill it up after each use, even if she only took two ice cubes out. He just liked a full ice cube tray. Again and again, she left unfilled blocks in the ice cube tray, and then they would fight! They would go rounds over this ice cube tray. He couldn't figure out why it was so difficult for her to take the thirty seconds it required to fill it back up. One day, he decided that actually it only mattered to him and it really was not worth all of the drama and fights, so he decided when he saw the ice cube tray had empty blocks, he would just fill it up and he would stop getting angry about the fact that he had to, because, after all, it only took him thirty seconds to do so. He would choose to love his wife by overlooking the fact that she didn't fill up the ice cube tray.

Oscar and I weren't even living together yet and we were having misunderstandings, but I remembered this story. I remembered that love wasn't always going to be emotional highs and fluttering twinges in my stomach, but it was going to be a lot about choice. And that choosing to love would become harder than empty ice cube trays and different uses of words.

I had spent five years plus countless summers studying and learning for my career. I'd endured low exam scores, written countless papers, and had read case studies into the early morning.

I'd spent my whole life trying new diets and working out for my body. I'd devoted time and effort to all of those things. And, while I slacked in the diet and exercise department, I never once gave up altogether on my body. Even when college was tough and assignments seemed impossible and I wanted to quit, I never would have actually considered quitting. I wondered why I so often considered quitting with relationship; with relationships, in general.

Why wasn't I willing to put that kind of effort into relationships with family and friends? Where did I ever get the idea that relationships would just magically gel, without effort, without going through the incredibly hard stuff and sticking it out? I wondered if this was maybe why the divorce rate was so high, why friendships often ended so terribly. I was willing to stick it out and persevere for all of the things that didn't really matter in the larger scheme of things, but was I willing to do it for people, for relationship? This was the best man I had ever met, and another man wasn't the solution. I loved Oscar more than I had ever imagined I could. But, I realized this was going to require effort for the rest of my life; and why wouldn't it? I wanted to be an expert in the things of business, an expert in the things of the Lord; I would need to be an expert on Oscar, and one day I would need to be an expert on my children. If I could study business strategies and methodologies, study how to grow as a leader, why couldn't I take time to study Oscar? Really study him. What made him tick? Why did he do the things he did? What made him utterly happy? What did I need to do to communicate better? How could I serve him? How could I grow in a way that would make my marriage a solid, fun, beautiful marriage? And, just as I failed at times during school, I would fail, he would fail, but I had to be willing to persevere.

Until I got engaged, I had thought I was a nice person and the best girlfriend in the world. When the pressures of a wedding and moving countries and marrying a man for life entered into the picture, though, I realized how un-nice I actually was. I also discovered the ugly stuff that was inside my heart. In Matthew 15, Jesus states that it's not what goes into a man's mouth that makes him unclean, but that which comes out of his mouth that makes him unclean. In Matthew 12 he also states that out of the overflow of the heart, the mouth speaks. The depth of my heart was ugly, and it was out of that overflow that I was speaking. Our pre-marriage counselors told us that every day we would be interacting with a person who was going to cause the deep things of our heart to rise to the surface. But, as those deep things came out and were dealt with, if we chose to deal with them properly, we would be made more like Christ. We were going to be challenged, we were going to be irritated, and at some point, we might ask ourselves why we married one another. We had to remember why we chose to marry the other and we would have to choose to love even when it was hard, even when we didn't want to, and even when it was easier to harden our hearts and become bitter and unforgiving.

On that picnic blanket in the park, after too many slices of pizza, I chose love; and I decided I would choose to love from that point forward. Oscar was a loveable man, a good man, a Jesus-man, but he wasn't perfect. Neither was I. God could write the most amazing love story, but we were human characters in that story: human characters with flaws, with issues, and with choices. If we chose to love, to serve one another and to delve deeper, our love would grow stronger and deeper.

My mentor told me once that marriage was like walking knee-deep in mud together. It was like walking-knee deep in mud, sometimes, but we'd be doing it together. I was also told by someone else that marriage could be the honeymoon that never ended, that we could keep the love alive, the fire alive. I prayed that when we were walking-knee deep in mud together, we would make it as if we were doing so through an exotic rain forest, the trees creating a picturesque canopy overhead. That we'd see ourselves as lovers on an adventure, journeying to an unexplored place, with undiscovered treasures. Lovers who would be closer and stronger at the end of our journey together.

Oscar and I got to a point where if we went an evening without fighting, we high-fived at the end. Our hands would meet in a head-level slap as we'd proclaim, "We didn't fight today!" We had to celebrate. We have to celebrate those moments when we choose to live up to a higher standard. We have to celebrate those little victories, because those little victories create larger and larger victories.

Oscar spent some days at the orphanage with me. We held and fed the babies and, as I watched Oscar interact with them, I grew more deeply in love with him. I watched the way he carefully and slowly fed the babies pea-sized amounts of food on each spoonful. I watched his anxiety surface when he got food on their faces and I watched him immediately wipe it away. I looked deeply into him, and I saw the intentions of his heart. I would have to keep looking for his heart, keep seeking out the truth of his intentions. He would have to do the same for me. Sometimes those intentions would be hidden behind unkind words and misunderstood actions, but the good intentions of that beautiful heart were still there.

One morning, as I laid the babies in their cribs for their mid-morning naps, I sat at the wooden dining room table at the orphanage. June is winter in South Africa, and I had made myself a cup of hot chocolate, because it was an unusually cold morning. I peered out the window and into the garden as I sat sipping out of my mug. Hot chocolate in June. I shook my head in disbelief. *This is my life now,* I thought. *This is just one small moment that represents how everything has shifted; how everything has drastically changed for me.*

During June in the States, I used to sit sipping sun-kissed iced tea, because there it is summertime. I had never really imagined anything different growing up, even though I'd had my daydreams.

Nothing in my life had happened as I imagined it would, and yet— even though it was difficult at times— everything that had happened had met my heart's desires. God is a radical God, I thought; a God whose plans didn't always seem to make sense and whose plans weren't always easy, but whose plans were perfect in His way. I said it again in my head: *hot chocolate in June*. And then, as if God whispered it to my heart, I knew I had just stumbled upon the title for my first book.

CHAPTER THIRTEEN

Where You Go, I Will Go

I VOWED.

"Oscar, you are the man I dreamed of, the man I asked God for, and I am so happy to be your wife-to-be, spending the rest of my life with you. You are strong, kind, loving, and you have a heart unlike anyone I have ever met. I love you. I promise to love you unconditionally for the rest of my life: through joyous times and through trials. I promise to respect you in your successes and in your failures. I will be faithful to you always and will submit to your headship as I submit to God. I vow to never stop learning about you, to be quick to apologize, and to always listen to your heart. God said it best in the book of Ruth, so let my heart echo this to you when I say, "Where you go, I will go. Where you stay, I will stay. Your people will be my people. And your God will be my God. May the Lord deal with me ever so severely if anything but death separates us."

On those burning granules of sand in my parents' backyard, on that sweltering day in July, Oscar held my gaze as he recited the vows he had written.

"Holly, my queen, these vows I say before God, family, and friends. I promise to be a prophet, priest, and king in our family, to seek the Father's heart, and to know the depth of His love for you. I promise you that these hands will hold you and never let you go. These arms will protect and watch over you, these shoulders will always be here for you to lean on, to cry on, and to carry you when you're weary. These lips belong to you: to kiss you, encourage you, and to always talk to you and never to lie to you. These eyes will admire you and be captivated by only you. These ears will listen to you all the days of your life. With these feet I will stand by you and will never leave you. And this heart will beat your name until it beats no more."

Our wedding was held, outdoors, on one of Nebraska's hottest days that summer. Our clothes and our guests' clothes were sticky with sweat. The heat was nearly unbearable, but I prayed that that kind of heat, that kind of intensity, would never leave our marriage.

On our wedding night, my heart was doing the flip-flops that my belly-dancing belly had never been able to.

"I love you, my wife," Oscar looked deep into my eyes.

"I love you, my husband," I replied, the uncontainable joy escaping in a glow whose burn I could feel rising in my cheeks.

The next morning we awoke early to catch our flight to the exotic island of Bali for our honeymoon. From there we would be flying directly to Johannesburg, so I hugged Mom, Jim, and my family goodbye.

Saying goodbye was difficult: even more difficult than my face revealed. It's an almost indescribable emotion to feel great sadness and great happiness in your heart all at the same time. There's a sudden growing up that happens all at once, as if you realize that there's always a sprinkling of underlying sadness in great joy. There's always something you're letting go of when you're moving forward. It's the realization of that letting go, of that loss, as well as the realization of what lies ahead, that creates the bittersweet feelings.

One of my best friends, Brynn, drove us to the airport. On the way, she was gracious enough to make a pit stop at a Starbucks, so we'd be fueled for the long trip. My first macchiato as a married woman! It didn't feel any different, though I sipped it in a more blissful state of mind than ever before.

We flew from Omaha to New York and then from New York to Hong Kong, where we had a layover. The Hong Kong International Airport is located on the tiny, man-made island of Chek Lap Kok. At roughly three miles long and two miles wide, the landing experience is nothing short of hair-raising. "If our pilot doesn't have his A-game on," I thought, "our plane might topple right off the end of this runway and into the ocean." The descent into the airport alone, with surrounding hills and the ocean on all four sides, was enough to make me want to stay in China.

"Oscar, we've got to tour China next!" I exclaimed.

"I agree!" he said, as excited as I was.

Approximately twenty hours after we set out from Nebraska, our plane landed at the Denpasar International Airport in southern Bali. Our tour guide met us at the airport and drove us to our hotel. On the way, we passed statues with contorted faces and bodies that sent shivers down my spine.

Our hotel was roughly a five-minute stroll from Sanur village and beach, where mostly middle-aged and older tourists stayed. Our tour guide informed us that the younger crowd, especially many young Australians, usually stayed in Kuta, a classic stop for backpackers. He offered to take us to Kuta, but we didn't mind the more relaxed and quiet atmosphere of Sanur. We checked into our honeymoon suite, which opened onto the pool and garden. The garden was elaborately landscaped with red and white plumeria trees, ornamentation, archways, and pillars of stone.

We quickly unloaded our bags in the room and set out on foot to explore the area and the beach, but we were immediately bombarded with taxi drivers raising their hands to form the ten and two o'clock position on a steering wheel, then moving them in a driving motion while saying, "Taxi? You want taxi?"

"No, thank you," Oscar and I replied.

"Maybe later?" each questioned in hope.

"Yes, maybe later," we replied.

After about seven consecutive "maybe laters," both Oscar and I felt like we should say something different, since we really weren't going to take all of those taxis later. Nonetheless we replied to each "maybe later?" with a "maybe later."

There was a massage parlor down the street from our hotel where a one-hour massage cost the equivalent of only five US dollars, so we spent two of our six afternoons getting a couple's massage.

In the village of Carangsari, at the Bali Elephant Camp, we climbed aboard a carved wooden seat that was saddled to an elephant. Our left side, and then our right side, was lifted and dropped, bumpity-bump, along with each giant step down the trail. It was no smooth ride, but then the best rides often aren't the smoothest. Later, in a tree-house-like café, with stunning views of the Ayung River valley below, we sat drinking coffee out of a mint green coffee mug, ornamented with an elephant's face. You know those moments when you think to yourself, "If we only do this, it's enough! If this is all we do, I will leave fully satisfied, fully alive!" It was enough. Soaking in that moment alone was enough.

For one day's adventure, Oscar had arranged for our tour guide to take us to a nearby coffee plantation. Oscar truly is a man after my own heart! Bali Pulina was not just an ordinary coffee plantation, though, but one where they use *kopi luwak*, a unique method of processing coffee. *Kopi* is the Indonesian word for coffee and *luwak* is the local name for a civet, a wild cat. These wild cats are real coffee snobs, who eat only the juiciest of the ripe, red coffee cherries, which are considered the best for brewing. While in the civet's stomach, the cherries are digested, but the whole coffee beans are expelled by the civet's digestive system. These beans are then collected, cleaned, and roasted, leaving a much more aromatic and less bitter bean. Our tour guide showed us the luwaks in their cages, as well as examples of beans that had not yet been cleaned and of ones that had. I actually got to visibly see ripe red coffee cherries! After all my years of coffee drinking, I still hadn't known that coffee beans were a seed that came from a coffee cherry! I don't know where I had thought they came from, but this was a revelation.

Kopi luwak is one of the most expensive coffees in the world, often retailing for $600 —yes, I said six hundred US dollars—per pound. Since we were in Bali, though, we didn't have to break the bank to drink some, as there it only costs about five US dollars for a glass.

Our tour package included a tasting at the coffee and tea bar. In clear, ribbed glass mugs were six different types of coffee and tea: lemon tea, ginger tea, ginger coffee, ginseng coffee, chocolate coffee, and Bali coffee. I looked across the coffee bar to my husband. I grew serious, studied Oscar's face, studied that moment, and etched it upon my heart. I thanked God for giving me a man who enjoyed coffee! I know it sounds silly, but I was wooed by God, and that moment of connection, of shared interest between my spouse and me, felt like it came directly from the hand of God.

Following our visit to the kopi luwak plantation, we visited the Ubud Monkey Forest. Monkeys lined the square, stone walkways in the forest, perched on walls and ledges, and hung from the trees overhead. We held bananas high above our heads and waited as the monkeys took off from their perches, climbed our bodies, reached up, grabbed the bananas, and then clambered back down.

The forest itself has temples scattered throughout it; in fact, there are temples scattered throughout much of Indonesia. To our tour guide's surprise, we didn't tour or view a single temple, but gently declined. We are living temples of our living God, so there was no need.

Northeast of Ubud, in central Bali, in the village of Tegalalang, are Bali's classic emerald rice terraces. Our driver slowed to a stop at the edge of the road; we stepped out of the car and gazed down upon those startling green staircases, looking as if they could lead us straight up to the Divine. Coconut trees surrounded the curved terraces, creating our own Garden of Eden with a unique beauty just as stunning, if not more so, than the vast ocean waters.

The workers in the rice paddies were merely creating sustenance on a challenging landscape: little did they know the beauty that God was creating. Centuries prior, hard-working rice farmers with primitive tools had begun carving the stepped terraces out of the steep hillside in order to plant rice. With what was before them, they made a way. Sure, plains and flatland would have been the ideal locations for their farms, would have been easier. But their labors had resulted in not only a staple food for the community, but in striking beauty that followed the contours of the natural hillside.

Today, tourists travel from far and wide to see the startling beauty found in a people's sustenance, in those stunning terraces. Perhaps this was a vivid picture of what God is always doing: creating—amidst our challenges—a striking beauty that we don't necessarily see at first sight. A striking beauty within us, a beauty which resembles His beauty; something startling that attracts people from far and wide.

As our honeymoon adventure continued, our driver weaved us through traffic to Pecatu village, on the southern peninsula of Bali. Steep cement stairs descended down a narrow crevice between two jagged rock walls. As the towering cliff walls merged closer and finally closed overhead, we climbed down and down and further down the pathway, as if descending into a cave. Finally, the sky emerged once more, and we found ourselves beneath a canopy of tropical trees. Like a young boy's early-morning hair, dangling trees sprouted from the cliffs at all angles.

More cement stairs led to the small, secluded, Padang-Padang beach. Standing there on this tiny beach at the base of the cliffs, we felt as if we'd stumbled upon a hidden treasure, a secret place of our very own; it seemed as if we could decide who to share it with, whom to introduce to its secrecy and beauty. We felt as if we were secluded, closed off from the rest of the world, even though tourists and sunbathers packed this not-so-secret place.

We tiptoed our way around the topless female sunbathers, my newly married husband shielding his eyes, and found our very own piece of beach, patched with seaweed and tucked behind a large rock formation. We sat in the shallow water, looking over the turquoise waters of the Indian Ocean. I'd been on the shores of this ocean before, though on the coastline of an entirely different country. On that day, three years prior, I had stood just out of reach of those crashing waves and in awe of God, chasing the dreams He might have for me in my mind's darkness—like catching fireflies on a summer's eve.

Once when I was a little girl, I caught a firefly and put it in a glass Mason jar. I added grass to the bottom and poked holes in the lid. I decided that this firefly was a girl, and I named her "Lantern." For the first couple of nights, Lantern's flicker replaced my plug-in night-light. As I drifted off to sleep, I imagined all the places she had flown to. Then I realized that if I kept her in that jar on my bedroom dresser, she would no longer be able to fly around the world, to see the world. Mom also told me that I couldn't keep her in there forever, because eventually she would die. But I didn't want to let Lantern go, because I was afraid she would die out there in that big ol' scary world. I was afraid a bird might swoop down and eat her, or another little girl might once again capture her but not love her or care for her as much as I did.

One evening, as the sun was setting in the sky, I opened the lid on Lantern's jar and let her flutter out, and I prayed that God would protect her. Every night thereafter, for a year or more, I thought of Lantern and where she might be. Every night I prayed that God would not allow a bird to eat her or allow her to get captured again.

Sometimes, as grown-ups, we still do that. Sometimes we reach out and catch our dreams like fireflies in the night sky and stick them in a Mason jar. They sit there, like lanterns before us. And we feed them and we nurture them, but because of fear, they remain locked up: locked up and never fully encountering the world.

This deeper knowing of God, this adventure, this husband, this paradise, was a dream I didn't even realize I had dreamed. I had dreamt of adventure, of the world, of a love I had never known. I had found that love in God. One of the ways in which He gave His love and those dreams to me tangibly was through Oscar, and also through the beauty surrounding me. God was allowing me to soar in this world, but I had to first open the lid to that Mason jar. When I did, I discovered that this world was good. This beach was good. This honeymoon was good. This husband was good. I was blissfully satisfied. God was indeed the giver of fullest life. God was good. He had been good all along, even in the midst of Dad's sickness and death; even then, He was the giver of fullest life.

Our honeymoon was coming to an end, but the honey, the sweetness, didn't have to end. Oscar and I vowed that even when it was tough, even if we got to a point where in our minds we thought we didn't want to be married, where we didn't even want to look at the other, we would work it out. We would tear down the walls in our hearts, the ones created to distance ourselves from one another when we were hurt by the other. We wouldn't let those walls, which could be built in a day, go up. We would fight for the honey; for the sweetness; for the fullness.

CHAPTER FOURTEEN

Café De La Creme

I WAS SHOCKED.

The culture of South Africa shocked me. It wasn't shocking to me in the sense that it was strange or foreign, it was shocking in the sense that I really didn't have a clue how to do things, and I had thought that I would. After all, I'd spent a lot of time in Johannesburg. But living in a place is entirely different than simply visiting there, I learned.

I moved into the roughly 325-square-foot, fully furnished garden cottage that Oscar was already renting. The lounge and kitchen were open-plan, so they flowed into one another. With no room for a table, a bar with four metal stools separated the kitchen from the lounge. A miniature bar fridge fit tightly beneath the counter top: there was no room for a larger refrigerator. There was no room for anything, for that matter! We called it our love shack and I loved our love shack, but this was not just my love shack: this was my new house! I was a new wife, and this was all the house that I had to set up?

Back home, I'd lived in a much bigger apartment—and it wasn't that big! I had had a lot of decorations that would have made our home feel like home. I had candles and shelves; signs and paintings. For a moment, I was saddened that I didn't still have these things. But as I looked around, as I looked at Oscar, I was more grateful to finally be with him. I was grateful for our house, because it meant that we had a house. And I was grateful for the lack of decorations, because now it meant we could pick them out together. We could build what we wanted to build; and we could do it together.

My new house was without my coffee machine, without my décor, without almost all of my clothes. My new house was without a large refrigerator, without air conditioning, without central heat for winter, without a dryer. I had to hang clothes on the clothes line—all year long. I had to iron our clothes; well, attempt to iron them. My kitchen sink only had one basin instead of two, and I didn't have a dishwasher. The hot water came out of one tap, the cold water came out of a second tap, so there was no mixing of warm water. I had to put the plug in the sink and run hot and cold water to create a decent temperature to wash dishes in. When I scalded my hands in the hot water, when I was so frustrated because I couldn't run warm water out of one tap, I would burst into tears.

This was no longer a temporary visit or a mission trip, this was now my home. I loved this country, but I hadn't known that it would be so hard to adjust to life here. I now called this African soil my home, but it wasn't my home: not yet.

For one thing, I couldn't find any decent Mexican food. In Johannesburg, there were hardly any authentic Mexican restaurants, and the few that claimed to be authentic really weren't. And even the largest of supermarkets in South Africa didn't compare to the Super Wal-Marts or Hy-Vees of the States. I could walk down the grocery aisles in the States and have a limitless variety in front of me. Sure, when I walked down these South African aisles there were some options, but in aisle after aisle I was shocked by how many more choices I had had in the United States. When I paid for my groceries, I had to pay for the plastic bags. This was to encourage customers to bring reusable cloth bags, or to return their used plastic bags. Back in the States, I could choose if I wanted to "go green." Here I could also choose to be more environmentally friendly—but I'd pay money not to choose it.

Options. I realized that, in the States, we were blessed with so many options.

Plus I was without a job, without a work permit, without a car of my own, without knowledge of where the post office was. Simple administrative tasks were a hurdle, such as mailing a package or figuring out the lay of the land, how the streets worked in our new suburb, or how to purchase airtime for my new phone. I was without understanding of how high my grocery bill should be. Was the cost of a certain can of soup outrageous, or was it reasonable? I didn't know unless I converted it to U.S. dollars, and even that wasn't accurate due to the different economies. Over the phone, I couldn't understand the accents of the people. I couldn't make out their words, and they couldn't understand mine.

I was dependent on Oscar socially—to introduce me to friends, to show me new places, to teach me how to properly drive his car: especially in suburbs I'd never driven in before. And our one car was a 1994 Toyota Conquest: that didn't have air conditioning, didn't have automatic windows or locks, and didn't have power steering. If I was sweating (and this was Africa), I had to wind and wind and wind and wind the window down. I was dependent on Oscar's salary, on his income. We could live on just one salary, but it forced me, it forced us, to make sacrifices to do so.

Suddenly I felt worthless. I felt as if I wasn't contributing anything towards our marriage or our life together. I had moved to South Africa to learn about a country, but the thing I was discovering about living in another country is that you often learn more about yourself.

In Wyoming, God had done a lot of work in me. I had learned so much about who I truly was and about my identity in Him, but there was much work yet for Him to do. I had unknowingly wrapped my identity around my hobbies, my interests, my career, my stuff, my ability to earn income, my freedom to go where I wanted to go when I wanted to go there. All of those things formed who Holly was and what Holly did. Holly sat at Starbuck's on Sunday afternoons. Holly bought Sara Lee brand low-calorie bread. Holly drove on the left-hand side of her car (yes, her very own car), on the right-hand side of the road. Holly worked to earn her own private income so she wouldn't have to be dependent on anyone else.

But when Holly landed in South Africa with her only belongings in a few suitcases, and a new home that was so very different from what Holly was used to, Holly's mind was suddenly assaulted with questions. "Who are you, really? Who are you, Holly? And what makes you who you are? Is it your career? Is it your ability to earn an income? Is it your ability to drive well and to know where stores are located? Are you defined by your lack of a large house, a dishwasher, a nice television, a clothes dryer, the decorations in your house? Does it matter that you have only a few clothes and shoes? Would you rather have time with your new husband while you're waiting to receive your work permit? Would you rather have time to spend with him, or do you want to give that time up while you work your life away to bring in the income to pay for all of the fancy stuff you gave up? Is that who you are? Who are you, Holly?"

Well, I learned who I was. I was a daughter of God. I was a woman, made in love, and filled with love to share. I was resilient, because I had a resilient God. I was patient, because He had given me patience. I was flexible, because God would never place something in front of me that would totally break me. I was beautiful. And that beauty wasn't created by my shoes or my clothes or my make-up or my weight. I was beautiful because my Heavenly Father delighted in me, and simply because I was His child. I am not yet a mother, so I don't know from personal experience how

absolutely delightful one's own children are, and simply because
of who they are, not because of what they do or don't do: simply
because they are one's own. I don't know that feeling yet, but I
imagine it's as close to the delight God feels in us as we can wrap
our minds around.

In South Africa, poverty was before me, every single day: at the
stop lights, begging for food, for coins, for clothing. Digging
through my trash can, scavenging for anything of value that
could be salvaged or recycled. I could only pour out my love for
others to the extent that I understood God's love for them, and to
the extent that I understood God's love for me. Life wasn't about
what I'd given up or about what I didn't have, but about what I did
have that I could give, that I could share.

I could forego highlights in my hair; I could forego fancy
coffees that I earned out of my striving and my effort. But there
was so much more I could do by loving out of my intimacy with
Christ and by praying for that intimacy for another. I didn't highlight my hair as often and I didn't drink fancy coffee as often.
But you'll find that my hair is dyed blonde again today, and I still
drink fancy coffees. They bring me small pinches of delight, and
sharing them with others brings me even more delight.

So sometimes I buy that domestic worker, who has never enjoyed a luxury coffee, a luxury coffee. Because I want her to know,
I want him to know, the lavish love of Christ—which can actually
be shared through a cup of coffee. I've watched the faces of these
individuals when they see the price, and I know they are calcu-
lating how many loaves of bread or how much pap could be purchased with it. And yes, they will get bread, they will get pap; we'll
help meet basic needs. But sometimes I want them to feel spoiled,
and to know that they're worthy of having somebody spend an

exorbitant amount on coffee for them just to treat them. And then I watch their faces—that face of first delight—and I listen as they say, "Mmmmm, that is so nice. Very nice. Very, very nice." Because there's One who paid an even more exorbitant price . . . for them!

There are certain things each one of us sacrifices, and they are different for each one of us. There are certain things each one of us picks up and shares, and they are different for each one of us. That's the beauty: the absolute beauty of life. That as we're sharing out of the love we have found, out of the joys and delights we have found, others are partaking and others are coming to know that Love, that Delight.

I can share countless stories about countless individuals who don't feel worthy of a gift, of a blessing. So often, when they're offered a blessing, they suggest something a bit smaller or something else that is "good enough." And that's great, and that's wonderful. But I want them to know—don't we want them to know?—that there is a God who doesn't just provide provision, but who provides exceedingly abundantly more than we can ask, think, or imagine. And it's not always in the form of the tangible, but in the intangible. And it's that intangible that will truly sustain them. That intangible knowledge and hope and understanding of how loved they are and how valuable they are; this will be their true sustenance. But sometimes it takes the tangible to teach the intangible: a tangible hug, a tangible blessing, a tangible look in their direction, a tangible prayer.

Fortunately, after I moved into our love shack, I very quickly learned not to focus on what I didn't have, but to see the wonder in what I did have. I found the wonder in hanging clothes on the line: because I got a serious arm workout while simply doing a household chore, with no need to go to a gym. The wonder I've found in ironing (though it's still forcefully found wonder!) is that I can listen to an entire podcast while ironing clothes. I can also put on a podcast while hand-washing the dishes, and so give myself the mental space to learn—without distractions. I learned the wonder that can be found in being scared to drive our car, and of having only one car, because it meant that during the days when Oscar took the car to work, I walked. I walked to the post office and to the coffee shops in the beautiful, subtropical South African weather.

And it was on one of those walks when I finally realized, on a much deeper level, the fullness of God's redemption, of His love, and of the amazing ways He can answer our prayers. That morning I went further than usual while exploring our neighborhood, and I stumbled upon a place that looked strangely familiar.

It was a quaint little building, painted an off-white, with floor to ceiling wood-framed windows. Maroon-colored awnings and signs hung out front. It seemed as if I'd been there before. In a dream, maybe. I stepped inside. I peered up at the large, vintage chandelier hanging from the ceiling. I looked to my left at the wooden tables, covered in white linen. To my right were shelves of cakes, muffins, baguettes, and baked goods galore. Floor-to-ceiling windows made up two of the enclosing walls, revealing the streets and shops outside. It was a cozy, homey little hideaway, a perfect oasis for enjoying some delicious coffee and a pastry with close friends, or while reading a good story. Maybe even while writing one.

Yes. Only three blocks from my new house, with my new husband, in my own little suburb of Johannesburg called Melville, was the De La Crème Cafe and Confectionery.

God had brought me full circle. This was where I had sat two years prior with Amanda, Allison, and Maria, a few days before meeting Oscar. Now here I was again, peering out the windows while dreaming big dreams, but this time knowing—without a shadow of a doubt—that the God who had brought me here is a God who actually hears our prayers—and a God who can bring our dreams to fruition.

I took a seat right next to the windows, one table behind where I'd sat on that day that now seemed so long ago. I ordered my coffee and sipped it slowly as the sun poured over my face, and I peered out at the streets and shops. I daydreamed, as I'd done before, and in my heart I asked God, "Why did you bring me back to this place today? Is there something you want to show me, something you want to remind me of?"

And it was as if God whispered back to me: "Holly, I brought you back here to remind you of the desires of your heart. To remind you of the dream you once dreamed, of the petition you once made—begging me to let you stay here, on this continent. I was the one who placed that dream in your heart, and I heard your prayer, and I brought it to fruition."

You've probably heard the French phrase *crème de la crème*: it means the creamiest of the creamiest; the smoothest of the smooth; the best of the best. So there I sat, in the De La Crème Café and Confectionery—in the best of the best of God's promises.

I was content.

For more information about
Holly Mthethwa
&

HOT CHOCOLATE IN JUNE
please visit:

Website: www.ruggedandredeemed.com
Email: Holly.mthethwa@gmail.com
Twitter: @hollymthethwa
Facebook: www.facebook.com/hollyrmthethwa

....

For more information about
AMBASSADOR INTERNATIONAL
please visit:

www.ambassador-international.com
@AmbassadorIntl
www.facebook.com/AmbassadorIntl